See Me After School

DEDICATION

To my grandchildren Matthew and Katy,
who, to me of course, seem perfect children,
and to my darling David and mother, Kitty.

See Me After School

Identifying and helping children with emotional and behavioural difficulties

Daphne Lennox

David Fulton Publishers
London

David Fulton Publishers Ltd
2 Barbon Close, London WC1N 3JX

First published in Great Britain by
David Fulton Publishers 1991

Note: The right of Daphne Lennox to be identified as the author of this
work has been asserted by her in accordance with the Copyright,
Designs and Patents Act 1988.

British Library Cataloguing in Publication Data

Lennox, Daphne
  See me after school: identifying and helping
  children with emotional and behavioural difficulties.
  I. Title
  371.9

ISBN 1853461636

Printed in Great Britain by BPCC Wheatons Ltd, Exeter

Contents

Preface   vii

Introduction   1

1 Definition and Classification of Emotional and
  Behavioural Difficulties   5

2 Approaches to the Aetiology and Treatment of EBD   15

3 EBD and Developmental Psychology   30

4 EBD and Environmental Stress   43

5 Absence from School — Truancy   56

6 EBD Associated with Physical Symptoms and Conditions   73

7 Psychoneurotic and Psychotic Disorders in Childhood   95

8 Child Abuse   116

9 Conduct Disorders   139

  Conclusions   160

  References   162

  Index   174

Acknowledgements

I would like to thank all my friends and colleagues for their support, especially my Professor, Peter Mittler, for his continuous encouragement and warmth.

Above all, I would like to thank my husband David for lovingly typing my script and proving to be a painstaking and imaginative editor!

Preface

As I planned this book it was with the aim of providing a simple reference book of emotional and behavioural disorders in children to be of use to a teacher faced with a disturbed and/or disturbing child in class.

I had been professionally involved with emotionally and behaviourally disturbed children for nearly thirty years and wished to share, with fellow practitioners, some of my experiences, both good and bad.

As the book progressed I realised that I had been somewhat naïve in my initial aim. Each chapter seemed merely to skim the surface of the area it aimed to cover and left as many unanswered questions as suggestions for solutions!

My original hypothesis, however, remained firm. When a teacher is able to understand a child, both as an individual and as an important member of his family and school system, he will be able to assess more accurately the special needs of that child.

The means by which these needs can be met will vary with the individual teacher, the resources available and the ethos and value system of the school.

It remains to be seen what the impact of the Education Reform Act, the National Curriculum and Local Management of Schools will have on the education of children with emotional and behavioural difficulties. As there is, to date, little hard data in this area, the subject has not been addressed in this book. This does not mean that the author does not have empathy with the headteacher and classroom teacher who are having to address the problem on a daily basis.

I can but offer my sincere support and admiration for those I know to be working so hard in this difficult field and to wish them all the fun and joy I have experienced in my career — in spite of the occasional frustration and heartache!

Introduction

Background

Since the publication of the Warnock Report (DES, 1978) and the implementation of the 1981 Education Act, children with special educational needs have, rightly, received more attention and, in some cases, more allocation of resources than formerly. Many education authorities have made serious attempts to integrate into mainstream education children with a wide variety of 'handicap'. As teachers, our awareness of what can be achieved with these children has been raised. Some buildings and classrooms have been adapted to accommodate children with a physical or mental disability; co-ordinators for children with special educational needs have been appointed within some schools; programmes of specialised teacher training, inservice, part-time and full-time, have been developed; different forms of support services have been created.

Amidst this laudable awareness of, and provision for, the special needs of an estimated 20 per cent of the school population (Warnock, 1978) there has been one sub-group of children whose special needs have been comparatively neglected – children with emotional and/or behavioural difficulties.

This observation is made from experience as a headteacher, from contact with teachers from a wide variety of schools and from an examination of the current literature.

Why has this neglect arisen when, as any teacher will confirm, children who experience painful problems within themselves and/or create problems for others are, like the poor, always with us ?

Several hypotheses, each with a ring of truth, present themselves as possible answers to this question: this group of children, often perceived as 'naughty', 'disruptive' or 'neurotic' does not inspire the same sympathy as a group of children with severe physical or learning difficulties; this group of children, because of the very nature of their problems which are often family based, does not have a powerful parent lobby; the ability to control a class has been the *sine qua non* of a good teacher and consequently teachers have been reluctant to admit that they are having problems with a pupil, and therefore have failed to identify such pupils and have felt self-conscious in asking for guidance and support in dealing with them.

As teachers, the first task is to survive, otherwise it is impossible to teach any of the children in the class. If survival entails the rejection of one particularly disruptive child this may seem a small and not unreasonable price to pay for the well-being of the whole class.

To that one child, however, this may be the last back-breaking straw in a long line of rejections from his family and society.

The hypothesis to be explored in this book is that a teacher, by learning to pick up the signals or cries for help which a child with EBD is sending out, will be able to respond constructively to that appeal. Thus, 'See me after school' may come to mean to a child who is anxious, angry or rejected that his 'special need' has been recognised by his teacher and that help and understanding are at hand.

Definition of terms

EBD – Emotional and Behavioural Difficulties

The early term for the children who are the subject of this book was 'maladjusted'. The Underwood Committee, who produced a report on The Education of Maladjusted Children (1955) realised that this term covered a diversity of 'problems' and therefore offered six sub-categories as follows:

(1) nervous disorders
(2) habit disorders
(3) behaviour disorders
(4) organic disorders
(5) psychotic disorders
(6) educational and emotional difficulties.

The generic term 'maladjusted', however, was still used most widely and children bearing this label were often educated in the same special school for maladjusted children, regardless of the sub-category into which they fell.

The Warnock Report (1978) and the rhetoric surrounding it rightly tried to do away with the labelling of children. In order to create a common short-hand, however, new labels have arisen, questionably better than their predecessors! Thus ESN children are now MLD children and mentally handicapped children are SLD children. Maladjusted children now bask in the somewhat science- fiction label EBD, i.e. children with Emotional and Behavioural Difficulties.

As this term and its sister SEN (Special Educational Needs) are now in common usage they will be employed throughout this book – with apologies to those who may, understandably, be irritated by them!

Unfortunately EBD, like its predecessor 'maladjusted', is a term which implies that all children who are thus labelled have similar problems and similar special needs. In practice this is far from true. The term may be used, for example, to describe a child who sits at the back of the class, totally withdrawn from peers and teacher; a child who plays truant or suffers from school phobia; a child who is disruptive or aggressive; and a child who exhibits very bizarre behaviour. Therefore the term EBD will be used in this book as an umbrella term only.

SEN – Special Educational Needs

The Warnock Committee, in striving to remove the stigma of the label 'handicap' when referring to children who did not conform to the 'norm', intellectually, physically, psychologically or socially, decided to describe children for educational purposes in the light of their *learning* difficulties, i.e. Special *Educational* Needs or SEN. Thus children came to be described as having mild, moderate or severe learning difficulties.

Children with EBD do, almost invariably, experience learning difficulties associated primarily with their inability to realise their intellectual potential until some of their 'problems' have been resolved. This co-existence of learning and emotional/behavioural special needs gives rise to a dichotomy – should the educational need or the social/therapeutic need take priority?

Traditionally, specialist teachers of children with EBD have tended to concentrate firstly on meeting the therapeutic need in order to facilitate effective teaching. This was highlighted quite critically in the DES Report (1989) on schools for children with EBD. As the 1988 Education Reform Act has given schools the legal obligation to provide a broad, balanced and relevant curriculum for *all* children, including those with EBD, the educational needs and rights of these children can clearly no longer be marginalised.

The use of the term SEN in this book therefore will be founded on the principle that educational, emotional and social special needs are interactional and interdependent. At any given moment a teacher may be asked to concentrate on one of these three needs but not to the exclusion of the other two.

By the same token, when suggestions are made for any disapplication or modification of the National Curriculum it is on the understanding that this will be temporary or relatively short-term as defined by the Act.

Structure of the book

Chapter One will examine the major psychological approaches to the assessment and classification of EBD and assessment techniques available to teachers. Chapter Two will discuss theories of aetiology and treatment. Subsequent chapters will examine specific forms of EBD as they present themselves in school. Wider implications of the presenting problem will be discussed in relation to the child, his peer group, teacher and family. The final chapter will, hopefully, imbue the reader with the basic optimism which the writer still feels after many years of working with EBD children!

By helping teachers to identify and understand the EBD children in their care it is hoped that they will then perceive the task of meeting emotional, behavioural and educational special needs as a demanding but rewarding challenge which can, at times, even be fun!

CHAPTER ONE

Definition and Classification of Emotional and Behavioural Difficulties

Introduction

As human beings we are insatiably curious about each other and are constantly seeking explanations for what we consider to be surprising or anxiety-provoking behavioural reactions or emotional responses from those around us. Hence our fascination with soap operas which thrive on titillating us with the unpredictable!

Teachers, in order to establish and maintain the control of a class which enables them to teach, need to be able to predict how each child in the class is likely to respond in a given situation. One of the axioms in teacher training concerning destructive confrontations between teacher and pupil, or the equally destructive apathy which can manifest itself in class at times, is to foresee them before they occur and take steps to prevent them. Children with EBD are often the least predictable children in class yet also the ones who generate the most anxiety within themselves, their peers and the teacher. What tools of the trade have educational and psychological research, theory and practice produced to enable the teacher to become a better predictor of children's thought processes, feelings and behaviour?

Turning to the existing body of literature for an answer we find that different theories of personality development, psychopathology and methods of treatment/education have been in vogue at different times. As Pervin (1980) expresses it, theories of philosophy, psychology and education have all been highly influenced by the 'Zeitgeist' or 'Spirit of the Age' in which they develop. In retrospect each era and each educational/psychological 'fashion' has contributed something of value to our understanding of children with EBD and the present Zeitgeist encourages us to adopt an eclectic approach and to draw on concepts which prove to be useful from each set of theories.

In this chapter, therefore, a variety of definitions, systems of classifications of maladjustment/EBD will be reviewed as an introduction to the understanding of children with EBD and the range of problems to be discussed later. The aim will be to enable the practising teacher to construct a flexible, eclectic and essentially pragmatic approach to the wide range of emotional/behavioural problems he may be expected to cope with whilst carrying out his teaching duties.

Definitions of maladjustment/EBD and systems of classification will be proposed as aids to a deeper understanding of children's special needs and not as rigid labels which a child will carry throughout his school career. Unlike physical and mental disabilities which may always remain with a child, though not necessarily as a handicap, EBD are often 'treatable' in the sense that they can be totally eliminated or dramatically reduced. It is vital, therefore, when working with EBD children, that any 'labelling' is seen as essentially temporary and is used to clarify the needs of the child and to indicate possible responses to those needs on the part of the teacher.

Whatever 'label' or system of classification we use to describe a child at a particular moment in time and in a particular situation, he or she is always primarily a fellow human being, worthy of our respect, affection and the best we have to offer as professional educators.

Sometimes it is extremely difficult to feel genuine respect and affection for a child who is creating 'hell' for us and for the rest of the class. We then have to make a decision as to whether, and how, we can cope with this child without sacrificing the needs of the other children. In order to have the confidence and expertise to continue to accept and integrate the child into the class it is helpful to have a theoretical framework concerning possible causes of the EBD child's difficulties for, as the French say. 'tout comprendre c'est tout pardonner'!

Just as different ages have favoured different explanations of human behaviour so will different teachers be drawn to different theoretical approaches. The author suggests, however, that, whatever one's personal bias, it is productive to open the mind to a range of possible explanations for each EBD child's complexity of special needs, which will in turn open the mind to a range of possible interventions.

The theories of aetiology and treatment presented in Chapter Two aim, therefore, to provide a 'menu' from which the discerning teacher may select what seems relevant and valuable at the time in relation to a specific child and his specific needs.

Definitions of maladjustment/EBD

Many of the early pioneers in the field of special education, when defining 'maladjustment', placed the emphasis on various causal factors, e.g. Lane (1928) on the stupidity of society; Bowlby (1953) on maternal deprivation; Dockar-Drysdale (1968) on the absence of satisfactory 'primary experience'.

Following the 1944 Education Act the Ministry of Education in 1945 defined maladjusted children as: 'Pupils who show evidence of emotional instability or psychological disturbance and require special educational treatment in order to effect their personal, social or educational re-adjustment.'

The Underwood Committee in 1955 widened this definition, stating that: 'A child may be regarded as maladjusted who is developing in ways that have a bad effect on himself or his fellows and cannot without help be remedied by his parents, teachers and the other adults in ordinary contact with him.' This committee touched on the temporary nature of the condition by saying that : 'It (maladjustment) is a term describing an individual's relation at a *particular time* to the people and circumstances which make up his environment.' Recognising that, as a definition, this was still too imprecise and narrow to cover the wide range of symptoms involved, Underwood gave six sub-categories based on groups of symptoms as follows:

(1) *Nervous disorders*
    These disorders are primarily emotional, e.g. the child who is persistently frightened for no *apparently* justifiable reason; the child who is excessively timid and shy, appearing to the teacher in class as apathetic; the child who converts his timidity and low self-esteem into an effusive, over-friendliness; the nervous child whose fears become attached to certain objects or rituals about which he becomes obsessive.
(2) *Habit disorders*
    These disorders are either concerned with failure to develop habits, especially to do with eating, sleeping and elimination, which are regarded as normal and appropriate at certain ages, or are disorders in which physical symptoms predominate, e.g.

allergies which are partly psychological in origin in that they are a response to anxiety.

(3) *Behaviour disorders*
These disorders are shown by children who are in active conflict not only within themselves but within their home, school and wider community. The behaviours range from temper tantrums to serious disorders such as cruelty, arson, stealing, persistent truancy, and sexual troubles.

(4) *Organic disorders*
In these disorders symptoms are produced by physical changes, usually in the brain or spinal cord, e.g. epilepsy.

(5) *Psychotic disorders*
This term is used to describe conduct which is so profoundly disturbed that it disrupts normal development emotionally, intellectually and socially. These are the children described as 'living in a world of their own', who often fail to develop speech and exhibit bizarre behaviours.

(6) *Educational and emotional difficulties*
These difficulties are not the result of low intellectual ability but are failures to learn through fear of learning or through playing the buffoon in class or through listlessness and lack of concentration. An underevaluation or sometimes an over-evaluation of actual ability is often present in the child.

These definitions, in their widest sense, produced by Underwood, still have much to offer, though many additional possible elements have been subsequently highlighted.

Moustakis (1956) linked personality into his definition of maladjustment maintaining that, when we speak of 'adjustment', we really mean a child's *personal capacity* for 'adjusting'. He noted that, in many cases, maladjustment is seen to be a failure to adjust to *adverse* conditions, yet the child is required to adjust and will be criticised for not doing so.

Eysenck (1990), in his research, also draws attention to the teacher's need to appreciate the relationship between a child's personality type and his behaviour and scholastic achievement. In the field of discipline Eysenck maintains that extroverts achieve best when a reward is in prospect whilst introverts need the fear of punishment to bring out their best. If this is the case, an inappropriate teacher approach to a personality type could result in a child being described, quite erroneously, as having EBD.

The Warnock Committee (1978) offered no new insights into our understanding or definition of children in this group.

Galloway (1987) rejected the term 'maladjusted' retained by the Warnock Committee and suggested 'disturbing' as a more accurate way of describing these children because they are the children who 'disturb' adults. There are some children, however, who suffer from severe emotional disturbance but do not in fact disturb a busy, harassed teacher because they sit quietly in class and cause no overt problems. Perhaps the definition, therefore, should be widened to 'disturbing and disturbed'.

The current and most widely used term, EBD, emotionally and behaviourally disturbed or having emotional and behavioural difficulties, embodies an acknowledgement that emotional difficulties usually affect behaviour and vice versa. With the proviso that criteria for using this term with its implied definition will be likely to differ from school to school it will no doubt continue to be employed – at least until a more imaginative and comprehensive successor takes its place.

Whatever the definition we choose to employ there is an implication that children in this defined group are in some way, however temporarily, 'abnormal'. This begs the question, 'what is normality?'.

Normal behaviour is behaviour which conforms to the 'norm', i.e. it is predictable and not unusual. Abnormal behaviour is deviant in that it deviates from the 'norm'. This is not a fool-proof definition, however, because it does not usually take into consideration children who appear abnormal due to an ability to be particularly good at something, e.g. to be gifted intellectually, artistically, athletically.

The culture, sub-culture and climate of the times are highly influential in establishing the approved standards, norms and expectations of behaviour at any given moment – witness, for example, the dramatic changes in the attitudes to sex, marriage, homosexuality and religion which have taken place in our British society over the last fifty years. Relationships between teachers and pupils have similarly changed dramatically over this same period within our culture.

It will also be realised that many behaviours construed as 'abnormal' are in fact 'normal' for a particular development stage, e.g. temper tantrums at two years of age, violent swings of mood during adolescence. Strangely enough, excessively premature early development, especially intellectual or artistic, is seen in a positive light, whilst slow, retarded development is labelled 'abnormal'.

Other behaviours, such as nail-biting or thumb-sucking, are only defined as an EBD when they persist over a long period of time or when they are very intense, e.g. when the nail-biter draws blood and the thumb-sucker distorts the growth of his teeth.

As already touched on by Underwood, other areas of malfunction may also contribute to the definition of EBD, for example:

(1) *Intellectual malfunction* – i.e. when there is a significant disparity between ability or performance affecting such areas as attention, concentration, comprehension, learning, memory, judgment and perception.

(2) *Emotional malfunction* – e.g. when a child experiences wild swings of mood or regresses emotionally and becomes overdemanding and uncontrollable or, conversely, becomes withdrawn and under-reacts to pain, either physical and/or emotional.

(3) *Interpersonal malfunction* – i.e. when the rights and needs of others are ignored or violated or when extreme fear or suspicion of others renders the child unable to make any normal social relationships.

Definitions of EBD therefore can be seen to be as numerous, varied and as complex as the range of problems they aim to define. Recourse to any definition, however objectively and flexibly utilised, must also take into account the context and environment within which the emotional disturbances and behavioural difficulties are taking place.

Classification of EBD

Systems of classification of EBD are also very varied and range from the beautifully basic, 'How can I tell the difference between the sick and the bloody-minded?' (Saunders, 1979), to the complexities of the multiaxial classification system embodied in the most recent edition of the American Psychiatric Association's *Diagnostic and Statistical Manual of Mental Disorders*, the DSM – III (1980). The latter system first classifies the individual child in terms of one of nine major psychiatric syndromes which he displays; next, it determines if there is any accompanying developmental disorder; third, the presence of any physical disorder that might be of significance is noted; fourth, the degree of psychosocial stress experienced in the previous year is noted; finally, the child is categorised in terms of the

Figure 1.1 Examples of symptoms loading on internalisation-externalisation for disturbed male and female children

Internalising symptoms		Externalising symptoms	
Males	Females	Males	Females
Phobias	Nausea	Disobedient	Disobedient
Stomach aches	Pains	Stealing	Lying
Fearful	Headaches	Lying	Stealing
Pains	Stomach aches	Fighting	Fighting
Worrying	Phobias	Cruelty	Running away
Withdrawn	Vomiting	Destructive	Swearing
Nausea	Diplopia	Inadequate guilt	Quarrelsome
Obsessions	Refusing to eat	feelings	Threatening
Shy	Obsessions	Vandalism	people
Vomiting	Fearful	Truancy	Truancy
Compulsions	Withdrawn	Fire setting	Destructive
Insomnia	Depression	Swearing	
Crying	Dizziness	Running away	
Fantastic thinking	Crying	Temper tantrums	
Headaches		Showing off	
Seclusive		Hyperactive	
Apathy			

highest level of adaptive functioning displayed during the previous year. It is an approach to classification which certainly provides for the diagnosis of EBD other than that reflected in the child's presenting problem but somewhat daunting to the average classroom teacher.

From my own experience and from my work with teachers, a useful starting point and one which is not over-powering is actually to start with the two broad categories, 'the sick and the bloody-minded', as identified by Quay (1984), i.e. those children who internalise their problems and appear fearful, inhibited and overcontrolled, and those children who externalise their disorders and become aggressive, antisocial and undercontrolled. Achenbach (1966) used a 91–item symptom check-list with 600 boy and girl psychiatric patients as subjects and from this he produced a hierarchical list of internalising and externalising symptoms as shown in Figure 1.1.

Quay (1984), in reviewing some 55 factor analysed studies of behaviour problems, found a total of seven behavioural dimensions that have been replicated in 10 separate studies. These seven dimensions (see Figure 1. 2) can still be grouped however under the broader heading of Internalising – Externalising syndromes.

Figure 1.2 Seven behavioural dimensions (Quay, 1984)

Behavioural dimension	Associated characteristics
CONDUCT DISORDER	Disobedient, defiant Fighting, hitting Destructiveness Uncooperative, resistant
SOCIALISED AGGRESSION	Has 'bad' companions Truant from school Loyal to delinquent friends Steals in the company of others
MOTOR OVERACTIVITY	Restless, overactive Overtalkative Excitable, impulsive Squirmy, jittery
ATTENTION PROBLEMS	Poor concentration, short attention span Daydreaming Preoccupied, stares into space Impulsive
ANXIOUS-DEPRESSED WITHDRAWAL	Anxious, fearful, tense Shy, timid, bashful Depressed, sad, disturbed Feels inferior, worthless
SOMATIC COMPLAINTS	Stomach aches Vomiting, nausea Headaches Elimination problems
PSYCHOTIC DISORDER	Bizarre, odd, peculiar Incoherent speech Visual hallucinations Strange ideas and behaviour

A useful starting point for the busy teacher who wishes to test out, quite simply and quickly, whether a pupil is rightly giving some concern over his emotional responses and/or behaviour is to complete Rutter's (1967) Children's Behaviour Questionnaire as shown in Figure 1.3.

Any item crossed in the Certainly Applies column scores 2, in the Applies Somewhat column scores 1, and in the Doesn't Apply column scores nothing. The scores are then totalled and a child scoring nine or over is likely to be experiencing some EBD. Sub-scores on the items with an *A* beside them indicate the presence of

Figure 1.3 A children's behaviour questionnaire (from M. Rutter, 1967)

Child Scale B TO BE COMPLETED BY TEACHERS

Below are a series of descriptions of behaviour shown by children. After each statement are three columns: 'Doesn't Apply', 'Applies Somewhat', and 'Certainly Applies'. If the child definitely shows the behaviour described by the statement place a cross in the box under 'Certainly Applies'. If the child shows the behaviour described by the statement but to a lesser degree or less often place a cross in the box under 'Applies Somewhat'. If, as far as you are aware, the child does not show the behaviour place a cross under 'Doesn't Apply'.

Please put ONE cross against EACH statement. Thank you.

Statement	Doesn't Apply	Applies Somewhat	Certainly Applies	FOR OFFICE USE ONLY
1 Very restless. Often running about or jumping up and down. Hardly ever still				
2 Truants from school				
3 Squirmy, fidgety child				
4 Often destroys own or others' belongings				A
5 Frequently fights with other children				A
6 Not much liked by other children				
7 Often worried, worries about many things				N
8 Tends to do things on his own — rather solitary				
9 Irritable. Is quick to 'fly off the handle'				
10 Often appears miserable, unhappy, tearful or distressed				N
11 Has twitches, mannerisms or tics of the face or body				
12 Frequently sucks thumb or finger				
13 Frequently bites nails or fingers				
14 Tends to be absent from school for trivial reasons				
15 Is often disobedient				A
16 Has poor concentration or short attention span				
17 Tends to be fearful or afraid of new things or new situations				N
18 Fussy or over-particular child				
19 Often tells lies				A
20 Has stolen things on one or more occasions				A
21 Has wet or soiled self at school this year				
22 Often complains of pains or aches				
23 Has had tears on arrival at school *or* has refused to come into the building this year				N
24 Has a stutter or stammer				
25 Has other speech difficulty				
26 Bullies other children				A

Are there any other problems of behaviour?

_____

Signature: Mr/Mrs/Miss _____

How well do you know this child? Very well ☐ Moderately well ☐ Not very well ☐

anti-social, externalised problems and sub-scores on the N items indicate neurotic or internalised problems. It is interesting to note that whereas some children will score dramatically more on one of the sub-scores, there are certain children who score highly on both.

A valid criticism of categorising is that the label applied to the child will undoubtedly have an effect on the way the teachers relate to him. Once a child has been classified as 'anti-social' or 'neurotic' all his behaviours and reactions are likely to be viewed as symptomatic of that label. Thus the angry response from a pupil who has been accused wrongly of some misdemeanour in class may be dismissed as 'typical anti-social behaviour' when it is, in fact, completely justifiable.

It is hoped, therefore, that teachers will only use systems of classification of EBD to guide them in their approach to designing constructive interventions and not to 'pigeon-hole' children into compartments from which they may never emerge during their whole school career.

Conclusion

In this chapter an attempt has been made to offer definitions and classification systems of EBD which will help the teacher to gain insight into a child's problems and thereby suggest lines of approach. It must be emphasised that this is offered not as a way of 'labelling' children but as a means through which a teacher may start to differentiate between the separate and often very different forms EBD can take and the very different special educational needs which ensue.

For detailed lists of criteria which accompany specific forms of EBD the reader is referred to the DSM 111 to which reference will be made throughout the book.

In time, the experienced teacher develops his own internal system of classification – 'that new boy Johnny just reminds me of Mark' – and draws consciously or unconsciously on his experience of what 'worked' with Mark to help the new boy Johnny. Formal definitions and systems of classification are simply conceptualisations of other professionals' research and experience in the field and should be viewed and utilised as such.

CHAPTER TWO

Approaches to the Aetiology and Treatment of EBD

Introduction

In special educational research each era has produced its own approach to the aetiology and treatment of EBD. In this chapter, four approaches will be examined briefly to form a 'starter pack' for the teacher who is keen to explore different approaches. Further material can be found in books devoted purely to the subject, e.g. Johnson *et al.* (1986).

The Medical Model

The earliest explanation of EBD in children was that these children were possessed by devils! This would be dismissed as mythological today yet, as recently as 1974, a thirteen year old girl suffering from hysterical paralysis had been taken by her intelligent, middle-class parents to an exorcist before finally being referred to the author as in need of special education!

The early more scientific approach to the aetiology of EBD was that these disturbances were caused by biological and physical factors. This became known as the 'Medical Model' and, as the term implies, was associated with doctors, symptoms and illness. The children with EBD were referred to as 'patients' and 'treatment' was often in the form of drugs. Stimulants were prescribed for children with hyperactive behavioural problems (Bradley, 1937), antipsychotics for the treatment of severely disturbed children, and antidepressants in the treatment of enuresis and childhood depression. Injury or damage to the central nervous system or the brain caused by illnesses like meningitis, accidents or shortage of oxygen during the birth process, were deemed to be some of the major causes of emotional and behavioural disturbance. 'Minimal brain damage', as demonstrated by irregularities in an EEG (electroencephalogram) was frequently quoted as the source of a child's behavioural problems but Werry, writing in 1972, maintained that the techniques available at the time were of untested reliability in discriminating between normal and brain-damaged populations thus, under the circumstances, the diagnosis of brain damage or dysfunction in the majority of children with behaviour disorders was little more than an enlightened guess.

The exclusively Medical Model of aetiology has long since been rejected as an oversimplification which does not take into account the complex interaction of biological, genetic, personality, social and environmental variables involved in determining human behaviour.

In the 1970s the use of drug therapy became unfashionable but an alternative biological explanation for behavioural problems was proposed in the hypothesis that allergies to certain foods and adverse reactions to certain food additives could be the cause. Shannon in 1922 had already described the dramatic change in behaviour of an irritable, cruel eight-year old boy when foods to which he was allergic were eliminated from his diet. More recent studies, e.g. Crook (1980), set out to prove that there is a direct link between food allergies and disturbed behaviour. Crook asked the question, 'Can what a child eats make him dull, stupid or hyperactive?' and arrived at the answer 'yes'. The studies have been criticised as methodologically unsound and yet there is continued interest, not least on the part of parents, in the influence of diet, allergies and vitamin supplements on a child's behaviour and academic performance.

Feingold in 1968 first highlighted the significance of food additives, especially the yellow dye, tartrazine, in the diet of children with behavioural and learning difficulties. He noted (1973) that the increased use of these additives over the previous twenty years coincided with the increased recorded rise in hyperactivity, behaviour problems and learning difficulties in children over the same period.

Methodologically sound studies, e.g. Harley, Mathews and Eichman (1978), have found, however, that it is a very small proportion of children who can be demonstrated to be affected by food colourings. Poor nutrition and particularly the use of excess sugar have been suggested by Charleton–Seifort et al. (1980) as an important factor in the development of behavioural and learning difficulties in children but research in this area, though promising, is still in its infancy and is by no means conclusive.

Humans are undoubtedly biological organisms and the degree to which our personality and behaviour are determined by our genetic inheritance continues to be argued and researched. Sociobiologists, like Lumsden and Wilson (1983), maintain that most of our behaviour is genetic in origin, whilst behaviourist psychologists, starting with Watson (1928) through to present day behaviourists like B.F. Skinner, maintain that all behaviour is shaped environmentally.

Current psychological theories tend to emphasise the *interaction* between nature and nurture, genetic and environmental factors. The concept that we are born with a genetically determined range of behavioural reactions (Gottesman, 1963), which are then stimulated or repressed by our environment, would certainly help us to understand how one child in a traumatic family environment may appear to weather all storms, whilst another child in the same family may be swept overboard and drowned.

As teachers it is helpful for us to be aware of the growing body of evidence for the influence of genetic inheritance on, for instance, intelligence, schizophrenia and depression, but in practice it is the environmental influences on behaviour that we are in a position to manipulate within the classroom and within the school system generally.

The psychodynamic approach

The psychodynamic view of the aetiology of EBD is similar to the Medical Model in that it views abnormal emotional and behavioural responses as symptoms of an underlying disease or pathology.

Such underlying causes must then be identified if the child is to overcome his difficulties and this involves providing, usually through play therapy, insight into past unresolved emotional conflicts which have lain buried in the unconscious. The psychodynamic approach to treating children was founded on the work of Sigmund Freud generally and his classic analysis in 1909 of a phobic child, 'Little Hans', in particular. Child psychoanalysis was later developed much further by one of his early disciples Melanie Klein (1932) and by his own daughter Anna (1946).

To the teacher in the classroom it is impractical if not impossible to offer any type of formal analysis to individual pupils. If, however, one accepts that an understanding of the underlying causes of a child's maladaptive behaviour can be important in our efforts to meet his special emotional needs, the following precepts may be of value:

- All children are born with strong biological and emotional needs for food, love, physical holding, security and outlets for aggression.
- The quality of the emotional relationship a child experiences from birth, in his family and later with significant others, including teachers, will be crucial in the meeting of these needs.
- Anxiety over unmet needs is a very important determinant of EBD.
- Changing the overt behavioural symptoms of unmet needs and inner conflicts is less important than dealing with the underlying conflicts since surface treatment may just result in a child substituting one symptom with another.
- Treatment involves providing insight into past conflicts unearthed from the unconscious.
- If a teacher as a 'parent figure' can allow freedom of expression, particularly through play, art and music, he may help the child to unearth these unresolved conflicts.
- If a teacher, without taking it too personally or feeling threatened, can allow a child to express the strong feelings of love and hate engendered by these surfaced conflicts, there is a possibility that the child may acquire insight and begin at least some partial resolution of these conflicts.

The teacher's aim, therefore, will be to help the child to find alternative, non-destructive ways of dealing with strong ambivalent feelings, e.g. by providing opportunities for the sublimation of aggressive feelings into sport or useful physical exertion, or facilitating the expression of loving feelings through a caring, helping relationship with the child's peers.

The psychodynamic approach to both the aetiology and the treatment of EBD asks essentially that the teacher of an EBD pupil tries to view the child's life through the child's eyes. The constraints of the classroom will not, of course, allow a teacher to give a child total freedom of expression within which to explore all his inner conflicts. Much can be achieved, however, if the teacher, as a significant adult in the child's life, can genuinely strive to tune into the child's needs and show his respect for these needs through the myriad verbal and non-verbal messages which flow constantly between teacher and pupil in the course of a school day.

Above all, the psychodynamic approach places importance on the role of feelings and emotions in determining how we think and how we behave. When a child expresses feelings to us in the classroom it is helpful not to discount or disparage such feelings but to accord them understanding and respect, however irrational such feelings may seem to us at the time.

A simple illustration of this in a classroom situation would be when a child who is achieving well for his age and is popular with his peers suddenly says, 'I feel that nobody likes me and I'm no good at anything'. The teacher might be tempted to dismiss this with, 'Of course you don't feel that, that's ridiculous!' Or he could just pause for a moment and reflect that there may be circumstances at home that could have triggered this response. Perhaps there has been a new baby sister at home and mother has been so preoccupied that the older child has felt temporarily neglected and consequently 'no good'. By allowing the child to express the mixed feelings that he has at the time about his parents and the new baby without condemning him, the teacher may provide the catalyst which enables the child to deal with these angry feelings which are, after all, in conflict with his love for his parents and new sister. Ambivalence in relationships is a difficult enough concept for an adult to grasp, so we should be scarcely surprised if our children need help in understanding it!

Behavioural approaches

Prior to the early 1960s most of those involved in the education of children with EBD had subscribed to the psychodynamic model of aetiology and treatment. Where emotionally disturbed children were being educated in small classes in special schools it was both practical as well as fashionable to adopt this approach. Within psychology and education simultaneously, however, there arose a dissatisfaction with the highly subjective, non-scientific ambience created by the psycho-analytic school. At this point the more empirically biased behaviourist approach came into its own. Not all children with emotional and behavioural difficulties could be catered for within segregated special education and teachers began to look to psychology for a more practical approach to the aetiology and treatment of EBD.

The behaviourists appeared to provide the answer. Their major hypothesis was that all behaviour is learned and that it is this learned behaviour which determines how we think and how we feel. The early behaviourist, John B. Watson, had in 1913 stated that, 'Psychology as the behaviourist views it is a purely objective branch of natural science. Its theoretical goal is the prediction and control of behaviour' – exactly the tool of the trade so vital to the classroom teacher. If unacceptable behaviours have been learned then they can, through the applications of the principles of learning, be unlearned and replaced by alternative, desirable behaviours. The behaviourist approach lent itself to rapid translation into techniques of classroom management which could be demonstrated to be effective, e.g. Ward (1971) and more recently, Wheldall and Glyn (1989).

The concept of the school, the classroom and the teacher as the environment which promotes and maintains the learning of certain behaviours, both desirable and undesirable, led to the introduction of programmes of behaviour modification to combat EBD. Most of these programmes were based on the 'operant conditioning' researched by Skinner (1953). In this approach desired behaviours, or to begin with approximations of desired behaviours, are rewarded, either with tangible rewards or tokens which can later be exchanged for tangible rewards, or with social rewards such as attention, praise and approval. In a process called 'extinction' undesirable behaviours are, as far as possible, completely ignored.

Two other techniques from the behaviourist repertoire proved particularly useful to the teacher. The first is known as 'modelling' and describes the process by which children can be encouraged to imitate the behaviours to be learned and those to be avoided. The psychologist Bandura (1977) has dominated the field in this research but teachers unfamiliar with Bandura's work will have used the technique instinctively when they have placed a 'naughty' child next to a well-behaved child or have drawn the class's attention to the dire consequences that befall a pupil who misbehaves.

The second technique of value to the teacher is that of 'systematic desensitisation' as explored by Wolpe and Lazarus (1966), in which the child is helped to overcome a fear or phobia by gradual exposure to the aversive stimulus. Imaginative teachers have intuitively recognised the need for this when for instance they introduce a child with little self confidence to a new piece of learning. In co-operation with parents and educational psychologists the technique can be particularly effective with children suffering with school phobia.

The behavioural approach to the management of EBD has made a vast contribution to the world of special educational needs in that it offers relatively simple explanations for those needs and is optimistic about the teacher's capacity to meet them.

If one accepts that many behaviours are learned and can determine how we feel and how we think, the following precepts taken from the behaviourist approach to the aetiology of EBD may be of value:

(1) Although it is obvious that all behaviours, including EBD, have antecedents which have shaped, caused and maintained present behaviour, the teacher can do nothing to change a child's early experience so he will find it more profitable to concentrate on present day observable behaviour.

(2) Most behaviours are learned as the infant and child responds to his environment – repeating behaviours which are rewarded, even if the reward is attention through being 'told off' or punished.

(3) If 'abnormal' or EBD behaviours have been learned, they can be unlearned and new desirable behaviours 'taught'.

(4) These new, adaptive, desirable behaviours can be taught through a process called 'positive reinforcement'. In this process the desired behaviours are rewarded with tangible, token or social rewards until they become incorporated into the child's natural repertoire of behaviours.

(5) The best way to eliminate undesirable EBD behaviours is to ignore them wherever possible, not even giving the child the reward of attention through punishment.

(6) Another way to encourage the EBD child to acquire a repertoire of acceptable behaviours is to use other well-adjusted children and oneself as teacher as models of desirable behaviour.

(7) If an anxiety, fear or phobia which a child displays over an object (e.g. a spider), an experience (e.g. going to the swimming baths), or a new task (e.g. learning a new mathematical skill), over-whelms the child irrationally, the teacher may seek to implement a programme of 'systematic desensitisation' (Lennox, 1982). The stages of such a process might proceed as follows:
STEP ONE – help the child to relax.
STEP TWO – introduce the experience in gentle stages e.g. in relation to the swimming baths' example, let the child watch others swim, initiate paddling in the shallow end in close proximity to a caring, trusted adult.
STEP THREE – proceed to simple swimming exercises, whilst remembering to pair each progressive stage with a reward that is meaningful to the child, e.g. staying behind after school, ostensibly to help teacher but in reality as an opportunity to have a private chat and receive some individual attention.

Above all the behaviourist approach to the aetiology and treatment of EBD is an optimistic approach in that it encourages the belief that behaviour can be helped to change and with that change will come a change in how the child feels and thinks about himself and in his ability to evoke more accepting and positive responses from his environment. It is an approach which is eminently practical in the classroom situation, and it can be immensely encouraging to a teacher who is often hoarse by lunch-time from shouting at his wayward EBD pupils to find that by systematically using praise and positive reinforcement, as an alternative to censure, he can achieve quicker results with comparatively less effort!

The behaviourist approach to classroom management has been dealt with very sketchily here but the author would refer teachers to the comprehensive body of literature, e.g. Harrop (1983) and Wheldall and Merrett (1987), for a detailed description of techniques involved.

The ecological approach

Unlike the psychodynamic approach or the behavioural approach the ecological approach to the aetiology and treatment of EBD does not look to unresolved inner conflict or to inappropriate social learning for an answer but to the interaction between a child and significant aspects of his surrounding environment, that is, the child's *system*. EBD results from discrepancies between a child's skills and abilities and the demands and expectations of that child's environment at any given moment in time.

Thus development of normal and abnormal behaviour is a product of all the aspects of the child's environment – home and family, culture and sub-culture, community and, not least of all, school. If we are to understand the EBD child in our classroom we must, from an ecologist's viewpoint, understand that child's experience of being in his particular family, neighbourhood and community, as well as his experience of being with us and his classroom fellows i.e. his *natural habitat*, (see Figure 2.1) or his *system*.

As Mittler (1989) states, the ecological model in psychology and education moves us away from the deficit or Medical Model of EBD, in which we looked within the child for causes of his disturbance, towards a more environmental approach with the school as one of the more powerful environments, for good or evil, of the child's formative years. The feeling expressed by Hewett and Taylor (1980) that the most significant breakthrough in the treatment of children

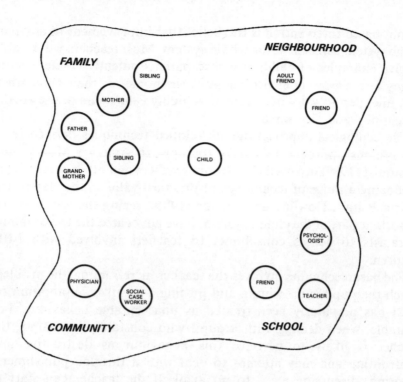

Figure 2.1 The child's system

with EBD has been the recognition of the vital role the school can play in a child's *system* has been reflected, particularly since the 1981 Education Act, in the move towards organising schools in such a way as to provide a 'whole school approach'.

Through a caring pastoral system and a well designed curriculum the effective 'whole school approach' prevents the child with SEN from being alienated within the school system and, hopefully, minimises his chance of failing to match with the demands of his school environment.

Once we have acknowledged with the ecologists that each child is inseparably part of a small social system and that, if he develops EBD, it is because of his failure to match the demands and expectations of this system, our aim in helping a child becomes clearer. The goal of any intervention we plan is to make the part of the child's system over which we have some control, i.e. the classroom and the school, work for that child so that there, at least, he no longer experiences 'mismatch'. The hidden agenda in this school-based intervention is the belief that improvement in any part of the system can benefit the whole system. Most teachers will be able to give examples of children whose parents patently create a more loving and accepting environment in the home for their child when they unexpectedly discover how he is highly valued and praiseworthy at school – and vice versa.

The ecological approach has developed techniques derived from the systems approach to family therapy. In America Molnar and Lindquist (1989) involved classsroom teachers and other personnel in producing a range of techniques of practical value in the classroom, and in Britain Dowling and Taylor (1985), seeing the school as an important part of the child's system, have advocated the use of family therapists to act as consultants to teachers involved with EBD children.

The basic technique involves the teacher in 'reframing' the problem which the pupil is presenting and putting a positive connotation on what has previously been treated as unacceptable behaviour. For example, when dealing with a pupil who constantly interrupts, the teacher is likely to perceive this behaviour as destructive and confronting and may attempt to deal with it through punishment, ignoring, discussion etc – to no avail. If the teacher can start to interpret the behaviour from the pupil's point of view, taking into account factors from the child's family system, he may be able genuinely to start to perceive this behaviour in a new light. The pupil, for example, may, by attention seeking at home, be unconsciously focusing parental frustration onto himself as a way of diverting his parents from the real family problem which is a breakdown in their marital relationship.

The 'identified patient', i.e. the attention seeking child, is in fact working very hard to maintain homeostasis in his family by constantly interrupting. Having perceived the child's classroom behaviour as a symptom of the family problem and not of the school system the teacher can offer to the pupil and his peers a new interpretation of his behaviour, i.e. that the child interrupts on behalf of the whole class so that the teacher can present more clearly the content of the lesson. He may even suggest to the child that in fact he should interrupt more often. In Family Therapy jargon this is called giving a 'paradoxical injunction'. A situation of conflict has now become a situation of co-operation in which the teacher has regained control without the pupil losing face. Changes within the EBD child himself, changes within his environment and the demands and expectations made from that environment, will all combine to create a happier system within which the child can adjust and flourish.

The ecological approach to teacher intervention uses techniques and methods from other models but in an ecological manner. The first goal may be to change the child's behaviour or, sometimes, to change the setting. At other times the priority is to change the attitude of those working closely with him and who perceive him as a problem.

Changes within the child himself may be accomplished through any of the techniques previously described, e.g. catharsis of strong painful feelings through creative play, used frequently with children who have been physically or sexually abused; programmes of behaviour modification to enable a child to develop new 'matching' skills in both difficult behavioural and learning situations.

Changes within the environment and its demands can certainly be engineered in the school and classroom. Firstly 'physical space', as discussed by Bednar and Haviland (1969) and Redl and Wineman (1952) can be manipulated to meet psychological as well as educational needs. The child with EBD should, in the classroom, be able to experience 'A House that smiles, Props which invite, Space which allows' (Redl, 1952:42). Areas where the child can withdraw safely for a short time when he is overwhelmed by demands he feels he cannot meet, or designated spaces where he can let off aggressive energy when he feels frustrated can all be provided in the school environment *if* deemed to be important.

All children, but especially EBD children, need the security of knowing where exactly they belong, i.e. their rightful classroom 'territory'. If as Laslett and Smith (1984) maintain, the good teacher always makes sure he is present in the classroom before the pupils arrive and that the arrangement of furniture is suitable for the lesson ahead, the physical environment will be used to its best advantage and form a 'comfortable' part of the child's system.

Other less tangible elements of the child's environment, his network of relationships in school, can be changed if the perceptive teacher considers them to be a negative or destructive part of the child's system. This may involve not only change in one's own attitude towards the unhappy or hostile EBD child in one's class but also the support and understanding of other members of staff. For example, a young boy who has been pushed into the 'man of the house' role at home since his father deserted his mother, leaving her with three even younger children, is facing well nigh impossible demands from that part of his system – the family. He may need, at school, to be relieved of this burdensome responsibility and allowed for the time being to carry less responsibility for his age in the class situation than would normally be expected from him.

Another important ingredient within the school child's environment is created by the demands of the curriculum. At a moment in history when schools are seeking to offer to all children the broad, balanced and stimulating curriculum demanded by the 1988 Education Reform Act teachers of EBD children find themselves in a dilemma. Post the 1981 Act the concept of a *relevant* curriculum became of paramount importance. This idea of relevance embodied the ecological principle that a school should have meaning to the daily life of a child and should equip him to cope adequately, not only with the demands of the school system, but also with the demands from his wider system and life after leaving school.

Where children with EBD were concerned it was considered highly important to include social, behavioural and 'life' skills as 'subjects' to be time-tabled and 'taught' alongside academic skills. Hegarty and Pocklington (1981) give an example of a curriculum offered to all fourth and fifth year pupils which would seem to be of particular relevance to EBD children who have suffered, almost invariably, some breakdown in relationships within their micro and macro systems. The syllabus quoted was divided up under the following headings:

- Making friends; finding out about yourself and other people
- Boy/girl relationships
- Sexual relationships
- Courtship, marriage and the family
- Development of moral sense
- Good manners; respect for other people and their ideas
- Class and racial discrimination
- Freedom
- Leisure – 'my time is my own'
- Provisions within the community.

Included in the concept of a relevant curriculum was the importance of the 'hidden curriculum' described by Galloway and Goodwin (1979) as including 'everything which is *not* formally taught, but which is nevertheless picked up in the form of attitudes and behaviour'. Thus the teacher who says 'we'll have no bloody swearing in this class' is most definitely contributing to the hidden curriculum!

How staff relate to each other and their pupils, how autocratically or democratically decisions are seen to be made and how the whole ethos of the school is created around certain priorities, will inevitably influence the value system of pupils and staff.

Teachers who place the needs of EBD children high in their list of priorities are naturally anxious that these may be overlooked when set alongside the high academic demands of the National Curriculum. If, however, we believe, as Warnock (1978) declared that, 'The purpose of education for all children is the same; the goals are the same, but the help that individual children need in progressing towards them will be different' we need not despair. We should be able with flexibility and imagination to offer the best of the National Curriculum without sacrificing their wider emotional needs.

If, as the ecologists maintain, the disturbed and disturbing child may be reacting quite appropriately to unreasonable demands from some part of his system are we, as teachers, in any position to offer constructive intervention other than within school?

Teachers are increasingly being asked to take into account the wider environment from which a pupil comes. In-service courses on how to identify and counsel children who suffer from physical or sexual abuse are now offered to teachers. Children who are homeless or have been taken into care of the local authority are known to us as are the home situations of many of our delinquent or disaffected pupils.

Though we may have no brief, resources or expertise to offer direct intervention other than within the school system we can, as teachers, legitimately contact, through the proper channels, other agencies such as Social Services, Health Visitors, Educational and Clinical Psychologists. I well remember a fourteen-year old EBD pupil of mine with whom we tried every therapeutic approach imaginable to help her to conquer her nocturnal enuresis – psychotherapy, behaviour modification through positive reinforcement etc, only to discover eventually that the real reason for her bed-wetting was to do with the fact that there was no in-door toilet at home and she was frightened to go out into the yard at night! When we contacted the local housing committee the staff were most sympathetic and an indoor bathroom was added on to the house. I was invited to the champagne official opening of the bathroom and the child's bed-wetting cleared up within three weeks!

Most local authorities are working towards closer co-operation amongst support services for children and families, in line with the requirements of the 1989 Children Act, and for teachers of EBD children the strengthening of inter-departmental bonds, particularly with Social Services Departments, can only be seen as a most welcome move. The teacher's task undoubtedly lies in adapting the school environment to the child's special needs but in doing so the teacher cannot ignore the demands being made on the child from other parts of his system. By fostering good relations with other agencies the teacher is well placed to provide a link for the child between his home environment, school environment and any relevant educational or social work support services.

If one is prepared to look at an EBD child from an ecological point of view the following precepts taken from this 'systems' approach to the aetiology and treatment of EBD will be of value:

(1) Each child is part of a small social system which has expectations about him and makes demands from him.
(2) It is not the child alone nor this social system which causes EBD but unharmonious interaction between the two.
(3) EBD may be defined as a disparity between a child's abilities and skills and the demands made upon him from his environment or parts of his environment.
(4) The goal of intervention, therefore, will be either to increase a child's skills or to decrease the demands from his environment – or a combination of both.
(5) Within the school environment the concerned teacher will try to understand the child's *whole* system and tailor his demands, within school, accordingly.
(6) The teacher, through the proper channels, will enlist the support of other agencies who may be in a position to make positive interventions in the child's wider system.

Above all, the ecological approach offers us the opportunity to view the difficult child not as a 'sick' or 'badly taught' individual but as someone who is responding, quite logically at the time, to unrealistic demands from some part of his environment. We are thus able to understand him more deeply and assess more accurately his real special needs. These needs having been assessed, the practising teacher is then able to draw on a wide range of methods of intervention. Furthermore, the teacher is then in a good position to mobilise other resources within the environment to bring about more harmony in the total system of the unhappy child's life.

Conclusion

From the wealth of literature produced by research, practice and theory in psychology and special education, a brief examination of the major issues concerning EBD has been attempted in this chapter.

Such theories have been viewed not as definitive in themselves but as starting points, from which the teacher might attempt to understand the disturbed and disturbing child in his class with the aim of providing the most effective and economic constructive intervention.

The psychodynamic, behavioural and ecological approaches to understanding EBD have been discussed separately but the author would like to stress that, in practice, the teacher is likely to draw on a combination of techniques from all three models and from many other approaches not discussed in this chapter. Most teachers will already be drawing from Piaget's theory of cognitive and moral development (1965, 1970,) and might wish also to look at Erikson's theory of psycho-social development (1963) and the counselling client-centred approach of Rogers (1961). For the teacher who is given the time and resources to work with children individually or in small groups the Transactional Analysis approach offers colourful and lively techniques, which are easily adaptable to the needs of children, Lennox (1982).

The skilled practitioner will, like Molière's 'bourgeois gentilhomme', who was delighted to learn that he had been speaking *prose* all his life, recognise that he has in fact been employing many of the strategies discussed. He will now, hopefully, gain confidence from the knowledge that not only has his teacher's intuition and experience served him well, but that he is well backed by an impressive body of academic theory!

CHAPTER THREE

EBD and Developmental Psychology

Introduction

When I, as headteacher of a residential special school for children with emotional and behavioural difficulties, used to interview the parents of children who had just been referred to the school, I always asked them when they had first started to worry about their child. The reply was frequently 'soon after he started school'. When asked if they had communicated this worry to any of the teachers their reply was often – 'yes, but I was told he would grow out of it'!

There is a range of problems that the child will not simply 'grow out of' and these are to be discussed in subsequent chapters but in this chapter some of the EBD which can in fact prove to be relatively short-lived or temporary, if recognised and handled with sensitivity and imagination, will be addressed.

Where life is confusing for the classroom teacher faced with 'difficult' behaviour from a child is that symptomatic behaviour associated with a serious, deep-seated problem can often appear, at a superficial level, to be exactly the same as the symptomatic behaviour of a child who is going through a temporary phase of maladjustment. These symptoms can include anything from regressive behaviour – e.g. wetting (enuresis), soiling (encopresis), thumb-sucking, extreme attention seeking behaviour – through aggression or withdrawal, reluctance to attend school or delinquent anti-social behaviour. By what yard-stick is the teacher to measure these behaviours and decide upon appropriate intervention?

The first rule of thumb test I always apply is to ask, 'Is this behaviour, however irritating, worrying or bewildering, 'normal' for the child's stage of intellectual, social, emotional and sexual development?'

It may be that it is only when we have been involved closely in the up-bringing of more than one child that we can be truly convinced of the validity of theories of emotional/behavioural stages of human development. The parents of most two-and-a-half-year olds may temporarily be horrified at the wilful, selfish, temper-tantrum throwing child they have produced, only to find that by three and a half he has become docility and charm itself. Similarly, those who are in close contact with adolescents will find the neurotic swings of mood and behaviour, to which these emerging adults are prone, infuriating and bewildering. If we can look back honestly to our own adolescence no doubt we were similar – yet here we are, sane, rational, stable adults!

As teachers we may have been versed in Piaget's stages of intellectual and moral development but, frequently, not so well trained in identifying the many other stages of development through which a child will pass on his journey to adulthood.

When we look at what the developmental psychologists have to offer as a guide to understanding 'normal development' in school-age children, we are once again faced with making choices. Do we believe, like Freud and the psychoanalytic school, that the early years are of vital importance in the development of personality and if so, do we maintain, like Erikson (1963), that if our earliest experiences have been less than satisfactory, it is possible to re-trace our steps at a later stage and, with the right input, 'catch-up' on our missed opportunities for psychological growth? Or do we favour subscribing to a hypothesis of recognisable and predictable developmental stages, through which a child will pass intellectually, emotionally, socially and sexually, in the manner he is observed to pass through predictable stages of physical development? Or do we turn to the behaviourists for comfort in their affirmation that, 'Except for elementary reflexes, people are not equipped with in-born repertoires of behaviour. They must learn them' (Bandura, 1977)?

For the purpose of constructing a framework of realistic expectations, within which a teacher may make appropriate judgments about the behaviour of children who fall within a particular age group, it is of value to take into account more than one theoretical approach and to view personality development as a continuous process in which the various stages are not discrete but usually overlap. Whilst accepting the premise that internal forces, i.e. genetic programming, appear to govern much of our development, there is always a strong interaction between this and external forces, i.e. differences in life experiences – the environment.

The framework proposed in this instance aims to encompass the following theoretical viewpoints:

- biological/ethological
- cognitive
- psychodynamic

Biological theories

Arnold Gesell, (1949 and 1956), one of the early developmental theorists, used a biological theory of *maturation* to explain why we all develop in similar sequences. This process of maturation is defined as internally determined patterns of change which unfold with age, are seen as being programmed in the genetic code and are relatively independent of external influences. For example, the hormonal changes at puberty that trigger the physical, emotional and hormonal changes in adolescents are part of a long chain of signals that appear to be programmed in the genes. Gesell in his clinical research demonstrated that psychological growth, like physical growth and motor development, follows definite stages alternating between those during which children are learning new things and expanding their personalities – e.g. from two years to three years and from 14 years to 15 years, when from a parent and teacher point of view children are 'difficult' – and those stages during which children are consolidating their 'gains' – e.g. from five years to five-and-a-half years and from 15 years to 16 years when children become more amenable and relatively stable.

The process of growth is seen as a progressive move towards independence and self-determination which can at certain ages and stages take the form of erratic, disobedient and acting-out behaviours and at other stages lead the child to look to his peer group for security instead of to his parents, e.g. in the gang activities of adolescence.

Figure 3.1 attempts to summarise the findings of Gesell in a way which provides a rough yard-stick for the teacher who wishes to measure a child's emotional and behavioural responses in school and decide whether a child's behaviour is 'normal' for his developmental stage.

The early biological approach to human development associated with Gesell (1945) and Barker and Wright (1955) is expressed today by the ethological school.

Figure 3.1 Ages and cycles

Stages	Cycle 1	Cycle 2	Cycle 3
A	1½ – 2 yrs	5 – 5½ yrs	10 – 11 yrs
B	2 – 3	5½ – 6	11 – 12
C	3 – 3½	6 – 7	12 – 13
D	3½ – 4	7 – 8	13 – 14
E	4 – 4½	8 – 9	14 – 15
F	4½ – 5	9 – 10	15 – 16

A Children tend to be relatively amiable and stable. They are happy to conform and present no discipline problems.

B Behaviour 'loosens up'; children become difficult and their favourite words are 'no' and 'mine'; in class they are likely to be disobedient.

C Children are relatively easy to manage. They seem happy to please the teacher and their favourite words are 'we' and 'yes'.

D Children tend to withdraw into themselves and display moody, anxious and introverted behaviour. They may well present in an apathetic manner and be hard to motivate.

E Children can now be motivated to learn and respond to humour from the teacher but may also behave in an expansive, boisterous way.

F Children achieve some balance between D and E resulting in behaviour that is more stable and self-sufficient. Once more, they should be a pleasure to teach!

As Cairns (1979) describes it, ethology is the study of the biological bases of behaviour including its evolution, causation and development. Children are perceived as members of a species born with a number of innate responses that are products of evolution – Darwin's process of natural selection and survival of the fittest. Ethologists believe that all these innate behaviours promote particular kinds of responses that will affect the child's development. For example, the 'hungry' cry of a very young baby, impossible to ignore, is a biologically programmed distress signal to promote feeding. The course of development within an individual follows a pattern that was acquired by the species because it ensured survival. Social behaviours, such as good communication and co-operation within relationships are as important as adaptive physical responses in the child's increasing repertoire of survival mechanisms and, by the time the child reaches school age, are usually quite highly developed and efficient.

If we observe that a child is notably lacking in the social skills compatible with his age and intellectual ability, we may question whether, at the critical point at which that skill would have developed innately, he was given the opportunity to express it. For example, children who all start life with very little capacity to 'share' or consider the needs of others, usually develop this capacity around the the age of four and, by the time they are at school, can engage co-operatively in activities with other children. A child who is severely ill and therefore over-protected and 'spoilt' at this age may have missed the 'critical period' (Lorenz,1966), for the development of this social skill and may need the teacher to give him 'lessons in sharing' to enable him to survive in his classroom peer group.

Similarly, if a young child has experienced a poor response to his signals, i.e. his crying, smiling and babbling, through being in a family where he is rejected, or through being cared for in an understaffed institution, he is likely by school age to show signs of severe developmental impairment (Tizard and Hodges, 1978). This may show itself in language and speech problems, displays of temper, hyperactivity and acts of aggression and destruction.

Fortunately there is a considerable body of research to support the theory that, although children who have suffered an emotionally 'impoverished' early childhood will present as having EBD, something can be done to redress the balance (Clarke and Clarke, 1976; Rutter, 1979). If the emotionally deprived child can be offered warm, trusting and stimulating relationships, both in the home situation and at school, the prognosis for 'recovery' and the development of pro-social behaviour is good.

When making a judgment about a child's behaviour, therefore, it is of immense value to the teacher to know if there is a history of emotional deprivation or damaging institutional care in the child's experience which may account for his failure to develop adequate and appropriate social skills and survival mechanisms compatible with his chronological age.

If this should prove to be the case, a caring teacher is in a strong position to make *his* 'institutional' relationship with this EBD child especially warm and accepting by, for instance, asking him to stay behind at the end of the lesson to help put some equipment away and then perhaps share a cup of coffee or just sit and chat. The use of positive reinforcement for any glimmer of co-operation and consideration for others on the part of a child whose emotional and social development has been arrested can quickly raise his self-esteem – and this, in turn, will have a positive effect on the way he relates and behaves towards others and, consequently, the way others respond to him.

Cognitive theory

The major contributor to the cognitive theory of development was Jean Piaget, whose work is usually studied in basic teacher training. To Piaget, children as they develop are explorers who respond to their environment according to their *understanding* of features in the environment. Understanding and interpretation of the child's environment will depend on his abilities, which are age-related and expand in complexity during the normal course of maturation (see Figure 3.2).

When we look at how Piaget viewed a child's emotional and behavioural development, i.e. his social and personality development, we find that he sees them as inextricably intermeshed with physical growth, maturation and intellectual development.

Thus, if we are to use Piaget's yard-stick as to whether a child's moral or social responses are 'normal' for his age and stage we would find that the child up to four or five years of age is **pre-moral** – i.e. he does not understand that rules in a game, for example, represent a co-operative agreement about how a game should be played. Between the ages of six and ten a child develops a strong belief in obeying rules, which have rightly been laid down by strong authority figures such as God, parents and teachers. This Piaget called the **heteronomous morality** stage. As parents we have all experienced our children at this stage vowing to us that what teachers say *must* be right! This time of **moral realism**, as Piaget also terms it, is when a child expects to be punished if his behaviour produces harmful consequences. A boy who accidentally breaks 12 cups whilst helping mother should still be punished more than a boy who breaks one plate whilst stealing biscuits.

By ten or eleven years of age most children are entering Piaget's

Figure 3.2 Piaget's stages of cognitive development

Approximate age	Stage	Primary schemata or methods of representing experience	Major developments
Birth to 2 years	Sensorimotor	Infants use sensory and motor capabilities to explore and gain a basic understanding of the environment. At birth, they have only innate reflexes with which to engage the world. By the end of the sensorimotor period, they are capable of complex sensorimotor coordinations	Infants acquire a primitive sense of 'self' and 'others' learn that objects continue to exist when they are out of sight (object permanence), and begin to internalize behavioural schemata to produce images, or mental schemata.
2 to 7 years	Pre-operational	Children use symbolism (images and language) to represent and understand various aspects of the environment. They respond to objects and events according to the way things appear to be. Thought is egocentric, meaning that children think everyone sees the world in much the same way as they do.	Children become imaginative in their play activities. They gradually begin to recognise that other people may not always perceive the world as they do.
7 to 11 years	Concrete operations	Children acquire and use cognitive operations (mental activities that are components of logical thought).	Children are no longer fooled by appearances. By relying on cognitive operations, they understand the basic properties of and relations among objects and events in the everyday world. They are becoming much more proficient at inferring motives by observing others' behaviour and the circumstances in which it occurs.
11 years and beyond		Children's cognitive operations are reorganised in a way that permits them to operate on operations (think about thinking). Thought is now systematic and abstract.	No longer is logical thinking limited to the concrete or the observable. Children enjoy pondering hypothetical issues and, as a result, may become rather idealistic. They are capable of systematic, deductive reasoning that permits them to consider many possible solutions to a problem and pick the correct answer.

stage of **autonomous morality** when children start to realise that rules are arbitrary agreements that can be challenged and even changed when it seems reasonable to do so. The child who broke one plate whilst stealing is now viewed as naughtier than the child who accidentally broke 12 cups whilst doing a good deed.

Kohlberg (1981) has refined and extended Piaget's theory of moral development into three moral levels and six stages of moral development as follows:

Level 1: Preconventional morality
STAGE 1: The child conforms to rules imposed by authority figures

in order to avoid punishment. If a child can 'get away with' something it is not considered bad. To many of the delinquent children we deal with the 'sin' is to be caught.

STAGE 2: The child conforms to gain rewards. By doing the 'right' thing the child feels he will benefit in the long run.

Level 2: Conventional morality

The individual strives to obey the rules set by parents, peers and social groups to win approval and maintain social order.

STAGE 3: The primary objective for the child is to be thought of as a 'nice' person who 'means well'. Moral behaviour is that which pleases – a form of 'good boy/good girl' morality.

STAGE 4: Behaviour is judged to be 'good' or 'bad' according to the extent that it conforms to rules that maintain the social order.

Level 3: Postconventional morality

This is the morality of self-accepted principles when moral standards are internalised and become the person's own.

STAGE 5: A morality of contract, individual rights and democratically accepted law. Moral actions are those that express the will of the majority or maximise social welfare.

STAGE 6: A morality of individual principles of conscience. The individual defines what is 'right' and 'wrong' on the basis of his own ethical value system and conscience.

From his research, Kohlberg found that 80 per cent of the moral judgments of ten-year olds were *preconventional* (stages 1 and 2) as opposed to about 18 per cent at age 16–18. Moreover, none of the 10–16 year olds in his sample used stages 5 or 6 reasoning.

Kohlberg argued that his stages of moral development are clearly related to stages of cognitive development but that intellectual growth does not guarantee moral development. A person who has reached Piaget's highest stages of intellect may continue to reason at the preconventional level about moral issues.

If we are able to accept this it makes it easier for us to understand the EBD child who is intellectually compatible with his age but presents as a moral 'babe', only able to keep the rules to avoid punishment or if offered some tangible reward. As Kohlberg explains, it is the combination of intellectual growth and relevant social experiences in the form of exposure throughout childhood to higher levels of moral reasoning that produces moral maturation.

When we say, in despair sometimes, 'how can you expect that child to behave differently when his whole family is amoral!' we are endorsing Kohlberg's view of moral development.

This would lead us back again to the relevance, particularly to the EBD child, of social and moral education as an important element in the school curriculum, especially at the secondary school level, when children can be exposed to and stimulated by discussion and argument which will help them to 'grow' and move towards a conventional level of morality at least.

Teachers, through sharing their value systems openly and honestly with their pupils, are powerful models, socially, morally and intellectually. Rutter *et al.* (1979), in their study of 12 London secondary schools, *Fifteen Thousand Hours*, found that children benefited from attending schools which set good standards and where the teachers provided good models of behaviour. Children also scored highly on measures of attendance, behaviour and academic achievement when they were encouraged to take responsibility and participate in the running of the school.

Psychodynamic theories

The major psychodynamic theorists all view the development of personality as taking place in stages. The teacher, brought up on Piaget's cognitive developmental theory of stages, may be easily receptive to the concept of developmental stages. The stumbling block when it comes to considering psychodynamic theory is the basic premise of Freud that children from birth are endowed with sexual instincts and energy. Freud saw personality as emerging from the individual's need to gratify an innate set of instincts, the most central of which is sex.

Traditionally, as teachers, we have concerned ourselves primarily with the cognitive development of our pupils but we are expected more and more to concern ourselves with the 'whole' child, to the extent of being asked to help to identify children who may be the subject of child sexual abuse, as well as of physical and emotional abuse. As inappropriate sexual behaviour is one of the clues to identifying victims of sex abuse, it becomes increasingly important that we are aware of what is 'normal' sexual behaviour in the age group of children we teach. The psychodynamic school of psychology offers one theoretical framework for making observations and judgments in this difficult area. Freud and his successors maintain that children, during the maturation process, pass through successive stages during which they focus on different parts of the body to satisfy emotional/sexual needs and to help them to discover their appropriate sexual identity.

Thus from birth to about two years the child passes through the **oral phase** when the mouth is the centre of physical/emotional/sexual gratification. Conflict or lack of adequate gratification, e.g. rejection by mother or mother substitute, may lead to a child later presenting himself, at school, as 'never satisfied', greedy, continually demanding and 'babyish'.

From two to four years of age the anal area is the centre of gratification. Firstly the child gains satisfaction, emotional and physical, from expelling faeces **(the early anal expulsive stage)** then, secondly, from retaining faeces **(the late anal retentive stage)**. Conflict at this stage may lead, in Freudian theory, to a child becoming too orderly and obsessed with routine and cleanliness or not orderly enough, i.e. defiant and obstinate.

From four to six years the child passes through the **phallic stage** when he/she becomes preoccupied with the genital area and the discovery of sexual identity. It is at this stage that the child's unconscious sexual desire for the parent of the opposite sex, the *Oedipal/Electral complex*, is expressed in his fantasies. The presence of sexual fantasies in young children can make it doubly difficult for us to know when a child is revealing facts about sexual abuse or is in fact describing fantasies. A teacher should have no hesitation in contacting resources with more experience and expertise in the field of child abuse, e.g.the specialist child abuse team in the local Social Services department or the NSPCC, when a child has chosen to reveal details of abuse to him about which he questions the reality.

Whereas the power of fantasy is strong in all young children, those who have developed some expertise in child abuse now believe that much of what children choose to reveal to trusted adults is in fact true (Peake, 1989).

The period from six years to puberty Freud christened **latency** – a rest period between the phallic stage and adolescence when there is little interest in sex and the child identifies with the parent of the same sex and enjoys the company of his peers of the same sex. Problems dating from this stage are usually a continuation of problems from the phallic stage, i.e. a lack of identification with the appropriate parent.

The final phase of development in Freudian terms is the **genital stage**, from puberty to adulthood, when sexual interest becomes focused outside the family and the young adult has the physical capability to act out his feelings towards others.

To the teacher looking for measures of normal sexual, emotional, behavioural development, Freudian theory is probably of more value in the nursery, infant, junior classroom than at secondary level. Most experienced nursery and primary school teachers are well aware that, for instance, children from two to four years invariably go through a very stubborn stage when 'no' is their favourite word, without ever having described it as late anal behaviour! In the same way, an interest in masturbation and in the genitals of the opposite sex is often highly noticeable in the child going through the phallic stage of development and games of 'doctors and nurses' need give no cause for real alarm if one accepts them as a 'normal' part of the child's psycho-sexual development at this age.

Equally the disgust displayed by both boys and girls at the idea of playing with the peers of the opposite sex during latency is accepted as perfectly normal in junior pupils.

For teachers of senior pupils the Freudian theory of development is valuable in understanding older children who appear to be fixated at a much younger stage of psychosexual development, e.g. the teenage boy who still appears to be unnaturally close to his mother, or the child who is pathologically mean and stubborn or is obsessed with seeking oral satisfaction in overeating, smoking or taking drugs.

For teachers, therefore, Freud provides a framework within which to judge a child's behaviour, particularly his sexual behaviour, in relation to his age and stage of development. If one can accept the basic premise that we are sexual beings from birth, Freud's theory of psychosexual development can provide us with insight when making a judgment about a child's potentially disturbing behaviour. For example, masturbation and sex play in four to six year olds will be viewed as a necessary phase which the child will indeed 'grow out of'. Similarly the preoccupation of adolescent pupils with members of the opposite sex will be accepted as perfectly 'normal'. A preoccupation with members of the opposite sex in a child who is still at the latency stage, however, *may* be indicative of sexual abuse.

The neurotic outbursts from the adolescent pupil who swings from moods of elation to moods of despair will be interpreted as a 'normal' stage in the child's maturation process and not as total inadequacy on the part of the teacher or indeed the child's parents.

Swings of mood and depression *will*, however, be interpreted as 'abnormal' in a young child for his age and should be further investigated – either personally or through the school psychological service.

Young children who indulge in frequent temper tantrums will be handled with firmness and consistency, as part of the normal process of teaching the child to recognise boundaries within which he can learn gradually to develop inner controls.

Senior pupils who display frequent temper tantrums and aggression are *not* reacting 'normally' for their chronological age and the teacher may need to investigate further. Is this anti-social behaviour symptomatic of a child who at the weaning, potty-training stage of development was never taught to accept controls? Is it regressive behaviour, which has been triggered by some traumatic experience in part of the the child's wider system? Is it symptomatic of inconsistent handling at home, where for example the child is constantly asked to respond appropriately to an over-indulgent mother on the one hand and an authoritarian father on the other?

The answers to these questions, if they can be obtained by the teacher, will determine the type of teacher intervention to be employed. For the child who experiences inconsistency at home the teacher will try to ensure that, within school, he experiences as much consistency of handling as possible.

For the child who is experiencing confusion, pain and anger at home, when for example his parents are constantly fighting, the teacher who knows about this may choose to devote some time, out of class, to allow the child to talk about his feelings and gain reassurance.

Conclusion

The concept of relating a child's behaviour to his developmental stage is not new to teachers. It has always been well known in school life that certain years, for example the fifth years, are the most difficult to handle, both from a control and a motivational point of view. When we are faced with behaviour that is disturbed/disturbing from a child it is worth making a mental check as to whether it is in fact perfectly 'normal' for the child's developmental stage – intellectually, morally, socially and sexually.

If the teacher has diagnosed the behaviour correctly as symptomatic of age and stage he will take appropriate action –

sometimes consistently firm and at other times more gentle and understanding – with the assurance and confidence that this is indeed something the child will 'grow out of'.

At other times when the emotions and behaviour of a child are *not* compatible with his chronological age the teacher will recognise that, without constructive intervention, the child will not simply 'grow out of' his problems and may need specialist help. Where there is suspicion of a serious problem, such as physical and sexual abuse, or extremely bizarre behaviour, the teacher should not hesitate to consult with experts through the recognised channels. Where the teacher feels confident that the problem is much simpler and amenable to a specific form of classroom management such as behaviour modification, he will proceed with confidence to provide constructive intervention.

CHAPTER FOUR

EBD and Environmental Stress

Introduction

Another form of EBD, which can prove to be temporary if handled with understanding and sensitivity, is the emotional and behavioural disturbance which comes as a direct response to a stressful happening or situation in a child's life.

In their interesting research into which life events cause most stress, Holmes and Rahe (1967) constructed a hierarchy ranging from death of a spouse to a change in sleeping habits (see Figure 4.1). What the research showed was not only a correspondence between stressful events and illness, but also the extent to which a number of not very high scoring forms of stress can be as important as one major event.

It is sometimes overlooked, and not least of all by teachers perhaps, that children are highly vulnerable in a stressful family situation and often feel totally impotent. Not only are they powerless to reduce the stress for themselves and other family members, they are also often unable to express their feelings appropriately or conceptualise their anxieties.

If we examine the hierarchy of disturbing events proposed by Holmes and Rahe, we would be unlikely to argue that these situations will not produce stress in the home and therefore(stressed responses and behaviours in the children we teach.

In this chapter, therefore, some of the stressful situations which will inevitably affect some of our pupils from time to time will be discussed.

Awareness and understanding of EBD in relation to stress at home

The vast implication for the caring teacher who wishes to identify and understand the child who is reacting to a stressful situation at

44

Figure 4.1 The life events chart

Stressful situation	Score
(1) Death of a spouse	100
(2) Divorce	73
(3) Marital separation	65
(4) Prison sentence	63
(5) Death of close family member	63
(6) Personal injury or illness	53
(7) Marriage	50
(8) Sacked/made redundant	47
(9) Marital reconciliation	45
(10) Retirement	45
(11) Change in a family member's health	44
(12) Pregnancy	40
(13) Giving up 40 or more cigarettes a day	40
(14) Sex difficulties	39
(15) Business readjustment	39
(16) Change in financial state	38
(17) Death of a close friend	37
(18) Change to a different line of work	36
(19) Change in number of arguments with spouse	35
(20) Pre-menstrual tension	33
(21) Large mortgage or loan	30
(22) Change in work responsibility	29
(23) Trouble with in-laws	29
(24) Change in living conditions	26
(25) Trouble with boss	23
(26) Giving up smoking fewer than 40 a day	21
(27) Change in residence	20
(28) Change in social activity	18
(29) Average mortgage or loan	17
(30) Change in sleeping habits	16

home is that he must, in the first place, *be aware* of what is taking place.

Throughout his nursery, infant and junior education, a child has ample opportunity to convey to his teacher the details of his home life. Which of us, as parents, has not been surprised, alarmed and sometimes embarrassed by the forthrightness of the family 'disclosures' in our young off-spring's daily or weekly diary for the teacher? There is a tradition in primary education of teachers getting to know the mothers and other relatives of their pupils — if only at the school gate — and therefore they are usually in a good position to know when a minor or major traumatic event has taken place in a child's life.

Senior schools with good pastoral care systems may also make it relatively easy for a pupil to convey, to at least one member of the staff, information about events at home which are causing stress. The sheer size of most secondary schools inevitably raises difficulties in this area.

If a child who normally presents as well adjusted starts to show signs of emotional or behavioural disturbance, the concerned teacher should be able to provide the opportunity for that child to communicate to him anything that is happening at home which could account for this disturbance. Here the ethos of the school will be of vital importance in creating an atmosphere of openness and trust between pupils and staff conducive to the sharing of anxiety. 'See me after school' can be interpreted by a disturbed child as either a call to punishment or as an invitation by a teacher who understands to talk about worries, however great or however trivial. What may seem to us, as adults, to be a very trivial problem may, to a child, appear enormous and we should respect it as such. Small problems to a child may be quite as 'big' to him as big problems are to us.

> I met a little elfman once
> Down where the lillies blow.
> I stopped and asked him why it was
> He never seemed to grow.
> He stared at me
> And looked me through and through.
> I'm just as big for me, said he,
> As you are big for you.

Common stress-producing events

Increasingly, since the 1981 Education Act with its emphasis on the integration of children with Special Educational Needs, the teacher has been asked to fill a teacher/counsellor role with disturbed and disturbing children. Once again we are seeking to see a child's world through his eyes so that we are truly sympathetic to the anxiety he may feel over, for example, moving house. Catching new buses or trains, changing school, making new friends, can all be highly stressful but, if at least one teacher at school is aware of the child's feelings and can spare the time to take an interest and provide reassurance, any disturbed behaviour associated with this stress can be relatively short-lived.

In their book *Your Second Baby* (1990), Patricia Hewitt and Wendy Rose-Neil write movingly of the life-long psychological harm the birth of a sibling can cause if feelings of sibling rivalry are not recognised and handled sensitively when there is an addition to the family. Dunn and Kendrick (1981) found that older children often receive less attention after the birth of a baby and they are likely to respond to this by engaging in attention-seeking behaviours both at home and at school.

Although, of course, it is the parents who are in the most powerful position to help the older child to perceive a new sibling as a joyful and enriching experience, a teacher who is in close contact with his pupils is able to re-inforce, through his personal experience of being a member of a family, and perhaps now having a family of his own, this positive approach to brothers and sisters.

However much parents try to conceal the facts about money worries from their children — and some families make no efforts whatsoever — children are nearly always sensitive to their parents' anxiety over money, even if ignorant of the real facts. Long-term unemployment, sudden loss of a job, trouble with mortgage repayments and other debts, are all highly stress-provoking factors, which will influence the feelings and behaviour of the adults in the family and, in turn, those of the children. Some children will appear hostile at school when requested to purchase something for a lesson, e.g. ingredients for cookery, which they know their family cannot afford. Other children may appear depressed and even refuse to come to school. There are schools where a 'whole school approach' is concerned with the 'whole child' and there is priority given to meeting basic needs, such as hunger and clothing, in a way which does not humiliate a child from a home where there are money worries. A cold and hungry child who arrives at school and is offered tea and toast and a pair of dry trainers and a sweater is likely to be infinitely more teachable than a child whose basic needs are ignored. The effort and money involved will be relatively small and if the school has an ethos of caring, neither the children nor the staff need feel self-conscious. The enlightened teacher is seeking to meet all of the needs in Maslow's (1968) hierarchy of needs. Such needs range from the physiological needs for food, warmth and safety, through the higher order needs to belong, to love and be loved, the need for self-esteem and esteem from others, through to the need to self-actualise and realise one's full potential.

One of the most alarming groups of children with unmet basic needs is the ever growing group of children from homeless families. Over the past decade, the 1980s, the official number of homeless families has doubled to more than 126,000. This accounts for 360,000 individuals and 164,000 children and does not include 1.2 million 'hidden' households which, forced to live with other families, stay off the official register. Substantial numbers of children without a proper home also go without an education, according to a report on the effects of homelessness by her Majesty's Inspectorate (DES, 1990). Where children do attend school their chances of doing well are slim as cramped conditions leave the children tired, listless and unable to concentrate. Permanent insecurity leads to stress and disturbed behaviour. The DES recognises that teachers often have no information about new transient pupils and that attempting to meet their needs can be demoralising. It recommends more co-operation between schools, local authority social services and housing departments. This type of co-operation is embodied in the Children Act (1989) and should rapidly become part of normal practice when dealing with EBD children. For a classroom teacher faced with such pupils there is a need for support from colleagues and an enthusiasm and ability to tap into whatever resources may be available to lessen the child's pitiful plight.

A less common cause of stress, though now recognised to be very disturbing when it occurs, is the emotional aftermath of a national disaster, such as the Hillsborough football disaster in 1988. Professor Yule of the University of London Institute of Psychiatry worked with children after the sinking of the school cruise ship Jupiter in Piraeus harbour in 1988. He found that only one teacher and one pupil drowned but at least half the children involved were still significantly affected after a year. Yule also found that children did not want to upset adults by expressing their feelings. Where there is a close connection between the community and schools, such as in Enniskillen where the Remembrance Day bombing occurred in 1987, children were encouraged and felt free to express their feelings. Many teachers, however, feel inexperienced and inadequate to deal with issues of life and death, mourning, grief and guilt, which are not perceived in many schools as a relevant part of the school curriculum.

Workers at the Hillsborough Centre are now developing an educational/counselling pack for teachers and Elizabeth Capewell, who worked with children in Hungerford after the 1987 shootings, has set up a Disaster Staff Network in Newbury, Berkshire to pool ideas and to give support to teachers faced with counselling pupils in this situation.

One-parent and step-parent families

Loss of a relative through a national disaster is uncommon but, sadly, 'absence' of one parent is becoming increasingly prevalent. Children born into a single-parent family may or may not feel that they are deprived but educational research supports the hypothesis that many such children do suffer emotionally and educationally. A study by the National Children's Bureau (1980), *Children in Changing Families*, found that children born into single parent families were, at the ages of seven and 11, less well-adjusted socially and under-achieving educationally, compared with a matched group of children who had been adopted as babies and with children born to two parents.

In an age when we like to think that illegitimacy no longer carries a stigma the 'fatherless' child in our class may still feel himself to be 'different' and his anger at this may express itself in rebellious 'I don't care' behaviours or in shyness and self-effacement. Equally the child born through artificial insemination by a donor, or adopted by a 'homosexual couple', may experience satisfying love and stability at home but cruel teasing from his peer group at school.

There has been much controversy over whether, as part of sex education, homosexual relationships should even be discussed in school. If one has, in class, a child from a homosexual background who is becoming disturbed emotionally and behaviourally, it would seem logical to afford that child some understanding and protection from a potentially cruel peer and staff group. By discussing, in the context of sex education, the possibility of there being more than one type of satisfactory 'nuclear' family, support can be given. By the same token, open discussion about the advantages of living in a stable, one-parent family, as opposed to an unhappy 'normal' family, may be possible with groups of pupils where the teacher's relationship with the group is one of empathy and trust.

Research into loss during childhood (Marcoux and Kielt, 1985) discovered that the loss in childhood of one or both parents through separation or divorce is similar to the loss experienced in bereavement. The children of divorced couples were found to be suffering from guilt and blame for the marital break-up and consequently were often seriously depressed and suffering from low self-esteem. These children also suffered from a significantly higher death anxiety when compared with children from a stable, two-parent family.

As the incidence of marriage breakdown is currently one in three it is highly likely that most teachers will have a child or children from such a breakdown in their class. In the acrimony which surrounds most marital conflict the child is often used as a pawn between warring adults and is likely to feel both angry and helpless. The guilt, depression and anger he feels may be expressed at school by anti-social attention-seeking behaviour or by emotional withdrawal and apathy.

Many children who have suffered the divorce of their parents also have to take on board a new step-parent and, possibly, step-brothers and sisters. Stephen Collins (1988), when writing from his own experience about step-parents and step-children, highlights the difficulties placed on children and adults alike in this situation. The child is torn between loyalty to his own, natural 'missing' parent and his 'new' family. It is not surprising, therefore, that jealousies arise and there is a new type of conflict within the home. Collins sees step-families as veering between two extremes. On the one hand there is a desire to deny that there are any problems in the new family and, on the other hand, a tendency to blame every problem, from major to minor, on the fact that it is a step-family. The fact that most 'natural' families experience problems from time to time needs to be stressed to children who feel heavily victimised by being in a step-family.

How can the concerned teacher, who has some inkling of what the EBD child is going through at home, react in the best interests of the child at school?

Once again if there is a trusting relationship between teacher and pupil the teacher may engineer an opportunity for the child to talk about his feelings. Sharing these feelings with an adult who gives him 'permission' to have strong ambivalent feelings towards his parents and siblings, but who can reassure him that with time these feelings will fade, can be therapeutic in itself.

EBD children, however, are usually very slow to trust and the teacher may need to provide less direct intervention than one to one discussion. The use of drama, especially role play such as the fixed role therapy advocated by Kelly (1955), can provide a safe vehicle for acting out painful experiences. The teacher does not need to interpret to the child what is being revealed through drama but it may help him to understand the child's world from his point of view. The use of video-recording can also be valuable in being able to re-play the scene and to highlight non-verbal as well as verbal communication. A family with whom the author was undertaking family therapy was video-recorded during the therapy session and then invited to watch the re-play. Throughout the session the mother and daughter had expressed, volubly, their hatred of each other. When the scene was replayed, however, it was strikingly noticeable that the mother and child, whilst expressing hatred, were holding hands. When they observed this they began to laugh and said, 'we can't hate each other that much!'

Assignments in art lessons can also give the child an opportunity to convey the way in which he sees himself and his world. Dalley (1984) suggests that art is a subjective experience, a part of a person's life and growth. An art activity, used therapeutically, can provide a concrete rather than a verbal medium through which a person can achieve both conscious and unconscious expression. The expression of suppressed emotions through art may, in itself, lead to a lessening of anxiety.

Music as therapy has also proved to be highly successful with some disturbed children. Fenwick (1986) states that the aim of music as therapy is to put the child's problem into a musical context in which inner conflicts are revealed and repressed emotions expressed. This is particularly valuable if the child has a natural aptitude for making music. Attention and praise given for his 'gift' can bolster the child's self-esteem at a time when his self-image is very low.

With younger children the use of play provides a safe 'arena' within which they can act out their disturbing family relationships. A flexibly constructed doll's house with family dolls, as made by Galt for instance, together with sand and water and dough, provide the raw materials for the child to construct for us his view of his world. This may enable the child to enact both what is distressing him and how he would like things to change. For example he may place the 'mummy' and 'daddy' dolls linked closely together and the child doll placed right outside the house, or in some isolated room ; or the child may place the child doll in bed with the 'mummy' doll and place the 'daddy' doll in a separate room.

Denis Stott (1982) in his book, *Helping the Maladjusted Child*, gives a graphic account of pupils who, feeling rejected at home by the loss of one parent, can bring their hostility into school and project it on to the teacher. Stott stresses that the teacher should not react angrily to this show of hostility, which is not directed at him personally, as anger would constitute yet another rejection to the child. This added rejection would reinforce the child's feelings of inferiority and of being unlovable, as in the poem of R.D.Laing (1970):

> My mother does not love me.
> I feel bad.
> I feel bad because she does not love me.
> I am bad because I feel bad.
> I feel bad because I am bad.
> I am bad because she does not love me.
> She does not love me because I am bad.

The sensitive teacher will not overwhelm the child by offering too close a relationship at this stage but will convey to the child that he is there and ready to listen and understand, whenever the child is ready to trust him.

Bereavement

The most extreme loss a child is likely to experience is through the death of a parent, sibling or close relative. The teacher may know the facts about a death in a child's family or he may suddenly encounter disturbed behaviour in a child who usually presents no problems. The bereaved child may show his grief and depression through apathy, withdrawal, nightmares, psychosomatic stomach aches or sickness. He may, alternatively, become extremely disruptive and attention seeking.

Young children may regress in their behaviour, e.g. by wetting the bed or being enuretic and/or encopretic even at school. Tatelbaum (1980), exploring the need for children to grieve, found that bizarre behaviour, both in and out of school, can start to occur when the grieving process is blocked. There can be a persistent extreme denial that the death has taken place or obsessive pre-occupation with fantasies of reunion. The child's academic performance may plummet and a bereaved child who does not withdraw into depression may suddenly become uncharacteristically aggressive and anti-social at school.

Sternberg and Sternberg (1980) suggest that teachers should be prepared for a delayed reaction from some children. They quote the example of one girl who, several years after her parent's death, suddenly in class began to weep uncontrollably as she had never wept at the time.

A child's understanding of death varies according to his age and stage. The pre-school child up to about five years of age does not see death as irreversible. Although he may have been to the funeral and is aware that the body is in the coffin, he assumes that the dead person will, for instance, still want to eat or to play.

Between the ages of approximately five to nine years, children do learn to accept that death is final but they personify death as a bogeyman or a monster who comes to get people, usually at night.

From nine years to adolescence death is no longer perceived as a bogeyman but as a biological process. Some children will explore abstract concepts about the religious or spiritual world.

For teenagers, death is one of the great universal experiences such as love and life. Whilst accepting that death is part of life they also fear it. Because of this fear they may try to defy it by reckless, dare-devil behaviour, for example by accepting dangerous 'dares'.

Not surprisingly many children experience new fears following the death of a close relative and Staudacher (1988) lists the most common six fears as follows:

- fear of losing the other parent
- fear that he or she will die too
- fear of going to sleep
- fear of being separated from a parent or sibling
- fear of being unprotected
- fear of sharing feelings with others.

One of the most common reactions of children to a death of a family member is guilt. They may in the course of 'normal' family interaction have wished the person dead. They may see the death as a punishment for their misbehaviour or they may feel that they had not loved the person enough. Intense feelings of guilt and recrimination dominate the child's life and need to be aired, understood and absolved.

Angry feelings are yet another reaction which need to be understood when the child becomes disruptive and aggressive, both at home and at school. The child feels angry, either at his own feelings of guilt or at his impotence in the face of death.

Van Eerdewegh et al. (1982) found that 50 per cent of their sample of bereaved children under seventeen were seriously affected in their behaviour and ability to learn for anything up to three years after the death of a parent.

Grief and grieving

Bowlby (1969) described a child's grieving process as taking place in three stages:

(1) The **protest** phase, when the child denies that death has taken place.
(2) The **disorganisation** phase, when the child accepts that the loss is irreversible.
(3) The **re-organisation** phase when 'letting go' of the lost relative takes place.

Tatelbaum (1980) discusses childhood grief in five stages:

(1) **Denial** or **isolation**.
(2) **Anger**.
(3) A **bargaining** phase, when the child who may be feeling guilty promises to be 'good' if the death can be reversed.
(4) **Depression**, when the child internalises his guilt and anger.
(5) **Resolution**, when the child finally accepts the death.

It is widely acknowledged that unless the natural mourning process is encouraged to take its course in adults and children alike, the scars left by the loss of a close relative can be there for life. One six-year old known to the author became increasingly disturbed after the cot-death of his brother. The parents, thinking they were being lovingly protective not to discuss this traumatic loss with him, unwittingly denied him the opportunity to grieve. When they finally sought counselling for their son it released the flood-gates of guilt, fear and anger and his behaviour gradually improved. Kubler-Ross (1983) describes this inability in some parents to facilitate their children's expression of grief very graphically.

The teacher's role

In a recent television documentary, following a day in the life of a big inner city school, one of the teachers, commendably, took the trouble to inform all relevant members of staff that a certain boy had lost a grandmother to whom he was very close. His advice to his colleagues was to *ignore* the boy if he kept crying in class. Is this the best that we can offer?

As human beings as well as teachers, we are often embarrassed by talking and listening to someone who has recently experienced the death of a much loved relative. It is almost a reflex response to avoid talking about the person who has died and of the painful feelings that are still around in the family.

In schools where discussion of death, grief and mourning are an integral part of the curriculum, it is clearly much easier for teachers and the bereaved child's peers to create opportunities for the child to express himself and to engage in the vital process of mourning. Hare *et al.* (1986), when discussing implications for teachers on how to respond to a child's need to grieve, stress that opportunities to help all children to understand the reality of death should be encouraged, so that when a significant death takes place the child has some understanding to bring to the situation. They further state that teachers should positively encourage a bereaved pupil to give expression to his feelings. Once again this can be achieved directly through the use of writing, painting and drama. Staudacher (1988) describes how friends of a teen-aged victim of an accident were helped in their grieving by an imaginative teacher who proposed that the class paint a memorial mural in honour of their dead friend. The students' painting reflected their personal relationship with the dead boy, as well as their view of death.

Very young children, or those with low verbal skills, can often discharge painful emotions and fears through fantasy in play. An older child, however, may derive more benefit from keeping a diary in which he expresses his inner-most feelings. Krementz (1983) quotes a bereaved adolescent: 'One thing that does help me a lot is writing in my diary because it is like a friend who will listen to you'.

Above all the teacher needs to acknowledge that grief and mourning are legitimate experiences and they may take a long time to work through. If the teacher has a pastoral care or counselling role in school he or she may offer a series of group counselling sessions with a group of bereaved pupils as described by Furman and Pratt (1985). In follow-up studies they found that 76 per cent of those who had taken part felt that their peers were the best people at understanding their loss.

Conclusion

At a basic level, the teacher who is confronted by a pupil experiencing emotional and behavioural difficulties which are the direct result of stressful happenings in his family system will find the energy required to offer some constructive support well spent. None of us can learn efficiently when we are pre-occupied emotionally and the 'message' contained within this chapter is that teachers are in a powerful position to alleviate, if not to eradicate, the suffering of some of our pupils. We can, through a personal, pastoral or whole school approach, provide the channels, direct and indirect, through which information about a child's circumstances can be circulated to all relevant members of staff. Our efforts, however humble, to understand and support a child under stress may help the stress to be as short-lived as possible.

CHAPTER FIVE

Absence from School — Truancy

Introduction

Many children with EBD make their problems felt dramatically by their *presence* in school. There is a group of children, however, whose problems only become apparent through their persistent *absence* from school.

School attendance in this country has been compulsory for over a century, and since the Education Act of 1944 the onus has been on parents to ensure that their children attend school regularly.

Reluctance on the part of children to attend school is not, of course, a new phenomenon — Shakespeare spoke of the 'whining school-boy with his satchel and shining morning face creeping like a snail unwillingly to school' (*As You Like It*, Act III). Laurie Lee in *Cider With Rosie* talks about his reluctance to return to school after his first day, when the 'present' everyone had talked about at the beginning of the day had failed to materialise! When I asked a group of forty students recently how many of them had never 'played truant' for at least one day in their school careers, only a handful raised their hands!

Many cases of absence from school are perfectly legitimate, for instance when a child is ill, or when there is a traumatic happening in the home, like a bereavement, or a family holiday which cannot be taken out of term time. When we refer to absence from school as a possible sign of EBD we are obviously not referring to these legitimate occasional absences. The true incidence of unjustifiable absence from school can only be approximate, however, in that some children may be absent because of an illness which has been psychosomatically induced or prolonged; and some children, from other factors within their family system, may over-react to, or fail to recover from, the type of disturbing experiences discussed in Chapter

Four. Their absence from school may indeed be a sign of emotional or behavioural disturbance.

Conversely, some children who are not in the least emotionally disturbed are kept at home to help parents to meet financial needs in the family, e.g. to look after younger children whilst both parents work. The traveller family for instance needs the financial support of the older children. As has already been discussed, children from 'homeless' families also find it very difficult to attend school regularly, as they move from one temporary accommodation to another.

Figures concerning the incidence of unjustifiable absenteeism, therefore, may tell us a limited amount about the true nature of the problem.

The most recent figures come from an on-going longitudinal study of absence being conducted, from 1980 onwards, in England and Wales, by Professor Gray and his colleagues at Sheffield University. Their interim findings state that there has been an average of 3,000 prosecutions of parents for their child's illegal absence from school and a conviction rate of 90 per cent. In 25 per cent of inner city schools there was found to be an average of 20 per cent truancy in fifth forms. HMI figures for 1988 found the average attendance figures in primary schools to be 92 per cent and in secondary schools 89 per cent.

These figures in themselves are alarming and serve to reinforce concern amongst teachers that pupil disaffection with school is on the increase. As Reid (1986) emphasises, although the peak of absenteeism is now amongst pupils over 14 years of age there are two other critical periods for the onset of school absenteeism, i.e. the last two years of primary education and the first and third years of secondary education. The kind of 'career truancy' described by Tressider (1986) may well have its roots very early in a child's school life, thus teachers of primary and early secondary school pupils are in a powerful position to take preventative steps if they are aware of potential problems in relation to attendance. Responsibility for reluctance to attend school has, until comparatively recently, been placed at the door of parental or social background. More recent research (Reynolds et al. 1980) has confirmed the findings of Rutter et al.(1979) that schools where attendance figures are good are characterised by a caring ethos, where there is good communication and co-operation between staff, pupils and parents and low institutional control.

Absence from school as a sign of emotional or behavioural

disturbance is usually subsumed under the two broad sub-categories of truancy and school refusal/school phobia, with truancy being classed as a form of conduct disorder and school phobia as a form of neurosis.

In this chapter, truancy will be discussed and factors within the school which may be significant in promoting or preventing absence from school will be considered alongside factors in the child himself, the family and the wider social scene. School phobia will be examined in Chapter Seven, which deals with psychoneuroses in children.

Truancy: a definition

The dictionary defines truancy as either unexplained absence from school or absence without leave or good reason, implying that this may be with or without the parents' knowledge or approval. More commonly, however, truancy, as opposed to school refusal, refers to absence *without* the parents' knowledge or consent and is regarded as one aspect of a wider 'conduct disorder' involving anti-social or delinquent acts (Galloway, 1986). Truancy, therefore, is often perceived as a social problem, as opposed to an educational problem. In fact the word 'truant' is derived from an old French word which means 'an assemblage of beggars' and the connotation of roguery remains.

We may from our *Tom Sawyer* or 'Enid Blyton' view of childhood picture the truant as a carefree, adventurous, cheerful, happy-go-lucky child, who just happens to have the courage to do what we all longed to do in fantasy. Most studies of truants, however, (e.g. Hersov, 1960) found that they tend to be socially isolated, unpopular, unhappy children who are low-achievers suffering from the reverse of the 'halo effect', i.e. the 'perennial rogue effect' — a far cry from the jolly japist or Tom Sawyer.

Social and family conditions and truancy.

Early research into factors accounting for truancy tended to concentrate on variables to do with the family and social background of the child, and evidence was produced to support varying social hypotheses. The evidence was at times also conflicting. May (1975) found that truants were drawn disproportionately from lower class families but Rutter *et al.* (1970) found no relationship between social class and truancy. Reid (1982) investigated seven variables to measure and compare the social background of truants with matched control groups and summarised these findings and those of other researchers in 1986 in *Disaffection from School*. Reid found that truants and absentees are likely to originate from families where some of the following conditions exist:

(1) The father is in unskilled or semi-skilled work or unemployed.
(2) The father may be away from home for long periods of time.
(3) The absentee is part of a large family living in poor, overcrowded conditions.
(4) There is marital disharmony, stressful abnormal family relationships or a one-parent situation.
(5) Parents are uncommunicative or unco-operative with authority or school.
(6) The child is in receipt of free school meals or involved with Social Services.
(7) The child lives in unfavourable rural or urban communities or conditions.
(8) The parents are the passive victims of a poor environment and are unsure of their rights.

Clearly the combined social stresses outlined above are likely to affect both a child's attitude to school and his academic performance and yet we can all quote instances of children from deprived backgrounds who have done extremely well at school and in later life.

Lack of support and interest on the part of parents of truants is cited as a precipitating factor in truancy. Reid (1983) found that 83 per cent of the truants in his sample came from families who had not visited the school in the previous year. If a parents's only contact with a headteacher or classroom teacher is to be 'told off' because his child is playing truant, it is hardly likely that a visit to school is to be viewed as a rewarding or worthwhile undertaking! Feelings of being 'unacceptable', of being a 'problem family', can all too easily be inadvertently reinforced by a teacher who sincerely believes that he has the child's best interests at heart by 'chivvying' the parents or threatening them with legal action over their child's non-attendance. A problem which may indeed have been precipitated by adverse social and family conditions can then become in addition a source of great emotional stress to the child, his family and to the school itself.

Poor attendance figures may, in the light of the Education Reform Act, be perceived as a poor advertisement for a school which has a vested interest in creating a good public image.

The classroom teacher may have little to no influence in improving the disadvantaged social or family background from which a truanting pupil comes but he can certainly help to minimise a child's feeling of social inferiority within the school. An understanding of the possible cultural conflict a child from a deprived neighbourhood may experience in school is essential. Mays (1954), in his classic study of Liverpool school children, illustrates how language and behaviour used in school may be in direct conflict with the practices in a child's home and sub-culture. The perceived middle class goals and value systems of some schools imply an undervaluation of working class values and provide little incentive for the low achiever from a less 'acceptable' social background to subject himself to daily humiliations, however subtle they may be. An imaginative teacher can, without compromising his own value system, be flexible enough to interpret a child's behaviour in the light of that child's social background. A child who comes from a sub-culture where swearing is quite 'normal' and acceptable is not, necessarily, expressing aggression when he swears at a teacher. Table manners, taste in clothes and even one's choice of newspaper, are not inherently 'good' or 'bad' but largely a question of up-bringing. By all means, as part of social education, widen the school child's knowledge of other cultures and socially accepted behaviours, but beware of endowing differences with value-laden judgments.

In a society which is becoming increasingly multi-racial an even greater understanding of a wide range of racial and cultural norms is essential if a teacher is to avoid causing unnecessary emotional and behavioural disturbance.

There has been considerable research into the learning difficulties of children from ethnic minorities who are struggling to become efficiently bi-lingual and the necessity of designing intelligence and ability tests which are not 'culturally loaded' has been quite well explored. Lowden (1984) gives excellent advice to teachers of children from ethnic minorities who experience learning difficulties. He advocates the use of criterion-referenced tests, as opposed to norm-referenced tests which have been standardised on a Western population, when trying to assess for example the special educational needs of an African or Asian child. Whereas a norm-referenced test gives us a score which relates to the norms of a standardised sample of children from a British culture, it tells us nothing about the Asian or African child's performance in relation to a similar cultural background. Criterion-referenced tests provide information about a child's strengths and weaknesses and what he still has to learn without comparing him to other children and, in the process, perhaps making him feel inferior. Having returned from a holiday in Barbados recently, the author commented to a West Indian student that she now knew what it was like to be part of a minority community — one white face surrounded by black faces. The student commented that it was nothing like the experience of being a black person surrounded by white people — the difference is black is 'bad' and white is 'good'! Megarry (1981), when writing about the education of ethnic minorities, uses the word 'minority' to refer not to 'relative numbers' but to the condition of being *inferior* or *subordinate*. The hypothesis being that ethnic minorities are distanced from the sources of power and status in the country they inhabit.

The psychological and emotional challenge for the child from an ethnic minority is to adapt to his present culture and succeed educationally and socially within it, without sacrificing the richness and tradition of his own race. When a child from another culture is showing signs of emotional and/or behavioural disturbance at school, which may result in reluctance to attend school, the teacher is advised to explore for a possible mismatch between the child's skills and abilities to adapt and the demands from the home, the school, or both.

Sometimes the solution appears simple, as for example when recently two girls from Muslim families were denied the right, demanded by their religion, to cover their hair during school hours. This special need could have been met and the girls prevented from absenting themselves by a straightforward adaptation of the school regulations.

Within the ethnic minority groups living in the United Kingdom there are, amongst themselves, feelings of higher or lower status. Research undertaken by the London School of Economics found that Indian and Pakistani pupils obtained better results in both the old O-level system and the new GCSE than Bangladeshi and Caribbean pupils. Feelings of academic inferiority are highly likely to lead to feelings of inferiority as a person in a school setting and it is not surprising, therefore, if a child from a low status ethnic background finds attendance at school to be an unrewarding experience.

Certain teachers and certain schools have spent time, imagination and other resources in trying to create an environment which develops the richness of the varied cultures represented in their school population. Striking a balance between 'over the top' positive discrimination and genuine equality of opportunity without patronisation is not easy to achieve. Children are gifted, fortunately, at picking up the real message a teacher is conveying and if that message is one of care and respect it should help to minimise the possibility of any emotional disturbance or reluctance to attend school that might result from a child's feeling of racial inferiority.

Questions of family, cultural and social background undoubtedly have some influence on a child's tendency to become a truant, though why some children from a similar background choose to truant, whilst others do not, remains something of a mystery. This now leads us to take a closer look at the truant himself.

The child who truants

A study of teachers' opinions of truants, conducted by David Farrington as part of the longitudinal Cambridge Study in Delinquent Development (1961 – 1973), showed that teachers found children who truanted to be lazy, restless and difficult to discipline in their primary schools and they took these characteristics with them to their secondary schools, where they were also seen as not concerned to be a credit to their parents, very untidy in classwork, lacking in concentration and frequently restless in class.

It is not surprising, perhaps, that in the light of the way such children are viewed by their teachers, truants have been found (Reid, 1982) to have significantly lower self-concepts than matched control groups of children who were regular school attenders! This begs the 'chicken and egg' question as to whether a child of low intellectual ability appears to underachieve, develops a low self-concept and consequently does not find it worthwhile to attend school, or whether the non-attendance at school produces the low achievement and apparent low intellectual ability. There is to date no convincing research evidence to extricate us from the circularity of this question. That truants do suffer from low self-esteem and that equally they are underachievers academically is not, however, in question. The classroom teacher is under a legal, as well as a moral, obligation to strive to develop each pupil's educational potential, whether his own political attitude to truants embodies a belief that the truant is a transgressor whose adverse experience of school is due to the pupil's own failings, or whether the truant is perceived as a courageous child who has the wit to see through society's biased system and to vote with his feet. It would be a useful preventative and therapeutic strategy for the teacher of a child who is starting to truant to spend time and effort in enhancing the child's self-concept. No matter how low the child's intellectual ability, he is likely to have skills, or latent skills, which can be reinforced and rewarded in a way which makes coming to school an enjoyable experience. If the child has few intellectual strengths he may have social skills such as the ability to support and encourage children smaller and weaker than himself, or the ability to lighten a heavy day by making the class and the teacher laugh. This is not to suggest that the child should be pushed into a clown role but that the ability to bring laughter and good humour into the classroom can provide a warm highlight in the day for a child who may feel almost permanently inferior in relation to his peers.

The importance of the peer group in a child's life, particularly in adolescence, is well documented. In a class group of high academic achievers the truant may well feel surrounded by peers whose value system is very different from his own. This situation, as Brown (1983) suggests, may prompt him to opt out of going to school and to seek the company of more like-minded peers. Fewer than one in five truants were found to truant alone.

Cooper (1986) proposed a model of the adolescent truant as someone who is failing to achieve the normal increasing independence from parents and has an inability to set realistic goals or tolerate frustration. The normal process in adolescence, which Cooper calls **desatellisation,** is most easily achieved through **re-satellisation**. This latter term refers to Cooper's description of the gradual replacement of the parents by the peer group as the socialising agent. If a child is rejected by, or chooses to reject, his peer group at school he is denied this re-satellisation process and is no longer motivated to attend school regularly. He will look for a more congenial peer group elsewhere. Hence the propensity for children who truant to form groups of like-minded peers who, with time on their hands, drift into delinquency and other forms of anti-social behaviour. Thornbury (1978) found that between 70 per cent and 80 per cent of the children he studied who had come into conflict with the law had begun by absenting themselves from school.

The prognosis for truants after they leave school is equally pessimistic as Surkes in an article in the *Times Educational Supple-*

ment (1988) points out. Data from the National Children's Bureau (1980) *Children in Changing Families* indicated that children identified as truants at sixteen go on to low status occupations, or unemployment, and are also likely to marry early, experience separation, divorce and depression.

This group of EBD children with their unendearing anti-social behaviours, in addition to their refusal to acknowledge that what we are offering them at school is a 'good thing', can easily become a group for whom the hard- pressed teacher feels very little empathy or sympathy. We would be less than honest and more than human if we did not admit that there are days when we are positively relieved that a certain disruptive, truanting child has failed to appear again!

Reid (1982) had found that the intelligence of persistent absentees was significantly lower than the 'normal' population and that they frequently needed extra help in the basic subjects. In Galloway's (1983) sample of truants 86 per cent had a reading age at least two years below their chronological age. Learning difficulties are rightly perceived, therefore, as a common problem amongst truants but, unless the teacher has access to the truanting pupil by somehow attracting him to attend school more regularly, it is impossible to offer him the remedial teaching of which he is clearly in need!

Whereas early research into truancy tended to focus on factors within the child himself and his family and social background, more recent research has also examined the role to be played by teachers and schools in the aggravation or prevention of truancy. These will now be examined in more detail.

School factors

In his examination of disaffection from school Reid (1986) found that truants themselves more often blamed factors in school for their truancy than factors in themselves or their families. Their dislike of school was associated with teachers, the curriculum and the running of the school. Many of the young people they interviewed felt that they were unfairly dealt with by teachers, considered as mere objects and treated according to how the teacher felt about them personally. They said that teachers took too little notice of what they had to say or how they felt and were culturally very different from them. They rarely lived in the same area as the child and both 'spoke different' and 'thought different'.

However, it is well known that certain children who might truant can be well behaved for one teacher, whilst being unmanageable or absenting themselves for most others. The relationship between teacher and pupil is clearly vitally important in the maintenance of happy, regular attendance at school. Paul Widlake (1983) describes a case of truancy in which fear of the teacher was the main reason for the child's absence. The boy came from a family where his father, who had subsequently left home, had been very violent. When the boy transferred from a predominantly female primary school to a predominantly male secondary school he began to truant. Unfortunately his fear of men was reinforced by the harsh physical punishment he received at school for truanting. Once again the need for the teacher of an EBD child to be aware of factors in that child's background is underlined. It is very difficult for a teacher to relate warmly and react sympathetically to a child who persists in perceiving him, quite irrationally it seems, as over-harsh and uncaring, unless that teacher has some knowledge of the child's emotional history. As has already been stated, the truanting, anti-social child is not always easy to like and yet he is probably the very child who most needs an adult to accept him and understand his special emotional needs. The teacher faced with a child like this requires accurate, relevant information, good support and co-operation from colleagues and seniors and needs to have well developed links with the support services of educational welfare and social services departments.

There are times, of course, when the perceived problem may need, in system's jargon, to be simply 're-framed'. Perhaps it is not the truanting child who is the problem but some aspect of the school life, such as the relationship between a pupil and a particular teacher, or even a particular lesson. If the teacher has the personal self-confidence and ego-strength to work through this relationship with the disturbed child, real progress may be made and school attendance become more regular. If the teacher is young, inexperienced or very personally threatened by the relationship, it may be more practical for him to seek the help and support of a colleague.

Gutfreund (1975) argued eloquently for the need, in teacher training, for teachers to be given the skills and sensibility which will enable children to open up and relate problems to them. Has teacher training in the 1990s made advances in this direction? The 1981 Act did certainly raise the awareness in the teaching profession of the special educational and/or emotional needs of up to 20 per cent of the school population and this in turn has had some influence on basic teacher training. There are also now in-service courses in Child Abuse, Drug Abuse, Management of Difficult Behaviour, in addition to the plethora of courses on teaching skills and the implementation of the 1988 Education Act. The development of multi-disciplinary teams to consider and take action on a complexity of social, emotional and behavioural problems is also producing direct and indirect training for teachers wishing to develop their interpersonal skills. This can only benefit the child with EBD including, hopefully, the child who truants.

Many truants, when asked about their reason for truanting, blamed what they perceived to be the *irrelevance* of the school curriculum. Whereas the 1981 Act produced interesting discussion on the relevance of curriculum generally to special needs (Galloway, 1985; Brennan, 1985), there have been relatively few studies of curriculum which specifically consider the relationship with truancy. Reid (1983) found that a larger number of truants preferred technical and arts subjects to the sciences and non-academic subjects. Subjects such as religious education and modern languages were perceived as irrelevant to their future lives and provided no incentive to attend school. In the survey made by Mitchell and Shepherd (1979) truancy was seen to be closely linked to dislike of school and especially the school curriculum. These findings were supported in an investigation into truancy carried out in three inner city schools in a northern industrial town. The children who truanted cited the lack of attraction *inside* schools rather than an attaction *outside* schools as their reason for deciding to truant. Many of the children also perceived the curriculum as too academic and too geared to the examination system. As we have touched on before, low achievers academically can lead teachers to have low expectations of these pupils which, in turn, leads to low performance.

It is generally accepted that many schools are organised in such a way as to give high status, and consequently high motivation to attend, to high academic achievers. Research consistently provides evidence (Hargreaves, 1967; Lane, 1990) to support this hypothesis. Certain schools, however, where attendance figures are above average, do not draw from a socially advantageous catchment area or take a high proportion of children with good academic potential. Whilst examining, with interest, factors in schools where there is a high level of absenteeism, it is possibly more constructive to examine factors in schools where attendance figures are good, in spite of certain potential negative variables such as poor teacher-pupil ratios and inadequate buildings.

If, as most educators seem to concur, it is the central aim of education to organise the school in such a way that *all* pupils receive education which will develop fully their *educational* potential, is it not of equal importance that *all* pupils should develop their potential for *social* and *interpersonal* skills? The ability to relate warmly and confidently to peers and adults is in no way to be confined to children of high academic ability — sometimes quite the contrary. Teachers, backed up by a 'whole school' approach, can sincerely represent to children a value-system which respects and values the 'whole child' and sees the school as a social institution in which each individual has an important part to play. The low academically achieving child from a disadvantaged family and social background can develop strengths and skills which will be highly valued and will make regular attendance at school a rewarding experience. Such strengths may lie in sporting or creative activities, in music, art or drama or the child may be, in spite of low academic success, a natural group leader or perhaps the person others turn to when they need social acceptance or emotional support.

Reynolds *et al.* (1980) confirm the research findings of Rutter *et al.* (1979) that the ethos of the school is important when comparing schools in the same locality with differing rates of absenteeism. Higher attendance schools are characterised by lower institutional control, less rigorous enforcement of certain key rules concerning pupil behaviour, good relationships between pupils and teachers and parents, the availability of incentives and rewards and the opportunity for children to take responsibility in the running of the school. All of these factors are amenable to modification by the *staff* rather than fixed by external constraints. It is within our power as teachers, therefore, to create the 'school that I would like' for most pupils — including potential truants.

Dealing with truancy

Measures which have been used or which might be used in dealing with truancy will be discussed under the following headings:

- legal measures
- school based measures
- use of other agencies and resources.

Proposed measures of how to deal with truancy veer from the sublime to the ridiculous! In the United States some schools have offered cash rewards to the pupils with the best attendance records (Gilchrist, 1977). Recently, in 1990, the British government came up with the suggestion that parents should forfeit a large cash indemnity if their child persisted in truanting — regardless of the fact that many children who truant come from poor economic backgrounds!

Legal measures

Parents of children who truant persistently may be prosecuted and fined or the child may be brought before the Juvenile Court, where poor school attendance can be used, in conjunction with other extenuating circumstances, as evidence for the child to be taken into the care of the Local Authority.

With the implementation of the Children Act 1989 in October 1991 the Care order formally imposed by the Court will be replaced by a one-year Education Supervision order.

Galloway (1986) had produced evidence that suggested that the legal sanctions at the time were ineffectual in producing better school attendance. A control group of truants, who were not the subject of legal action, steadily improved their attendance, although they had initially truanted as persistently as the two court samples. Galloway also found that there were no clear criteria being used for the use of legal sanctions.

Berg (1980), when reporting a controlled experiment carried out in Leeds, found that children whose cases were adjourned by the Juvenile court for further consideration tended to resume attendance at school more quickly than a similar group who had been put under supervision orders.

Legal action in itself appears to have minimal effectiveness, particularly where its side effects for the child and his family are concerned. A child who is forced back to school as the result of court procedures is likely to react in an emotionally and/or behaviourally disturbed way, unless the motivation for his truancy has been understood. Taylor, Lacy and Bracken (1979) observed in their research that courts were unwilling to accept any defence by the truant which cited the inadequacy or inappropriateness of the curriculum and form of education which was being offered at school. Though many local education authorities would state that they use legal sanctions only as a last resort there are still a number of children taken into care on the grounds of truancy. The effect of this institutionalisation, without good reasons to maintain that the child is at grave risk if left in his own home, can be devastating. Happily, the Children Act 1989 has now addressed this problem.

The use of legal sanctions, therefore, is likely to decrease steadily over the next few years. As teachers, dealing with truants, the ball is being thrown back into our court. What steps can we take in school both to prevent truancy or, when it has occurred, to provide positive and realistic ways of dealing with it?

School based measures

As our discussion of the role of the teacher and the whole ethos of the school has implied, the most effective measure concerning truancy is to take steps to prevent it or to curb it at a very early stage. Reid (1984) feels that it is most important for a school's pastoral care team to spend time and energy in following up initial non-attendance. Parents should be interviewed and invited into school in a non-threatening manner and random as well as scheduled checks on attendance should be carried out.

At the same time, as is true with the treatment of most forms of EBD, positive reinforcement of the desired behaviour is more effective than punishment. Fear of punishment, if the child does return to school, is highly likely to deter the truant from returning. Further absence and the knowledge that he will be even further 'behind' in his studies, combined with a fear of punishment, will reinforce his need to truant, thus setting up a vicious circle. If good attendance is systematically rewarded with, for instance, an end of term trip or some tangible object or experience which is meaningful to the pupil and/or class, a pattern of persistent truancy is less likely to become established.

It is important that each pupil feels that at least one teacher in school not only knows when he is present or absent but actually *cares*. The truant may have started to absent himself through problems ranging from fear of being bullied, to fear of academic inadequacy, to problems of school uniform or personal problems such as head lice, dirty clothes and even 'unfashionable' trainers. If there is at least one teacher in school with whom he can talk, in confidence, with the knowledge that how he feels will not be scorned, this may make all the difference to his willingness to attend school. The need to have a whole school policy towards the prevention of truancy and the measures to be taken, with which every member of staff is familiar, would seem obvious.

In a survey of the techniques used in one school to combat absenteeism it was found that intervention strategies seemed to be selected at random and that there was no apparent planned progression of treatment. Fifteen specific treatments were identified but no record was kept as to their effectiveness!

The peak times for truancy identified by Tresidder (1986) were Christmas week and the last few weeks of the summer term, although absence seemed to increase steadily throughout the year. This would seem to suggest that certain pupils start each year and term with high hopes and expectations which are not realised.

Quite obviously, if a child who is likely to become a persistent truant can be identified in his primary school any constructive intervention undertaken by his teachers and the school will be of value in discouraging him from becoming a 'career truant'. In Reid's (1982) sample, for instance, nearly 20 per cent of the persistent absentees first began to miss school at the Junior stage. Teachers in primary schools are in an ideal position to respond to the special needs of potential truants in that they do not, traditionally, have to cope with the pastoral, academic dichotomy, sometimes enforced on teachers within secondary education. The primary school teacher has contact with the same pupils for most of the day and is therefore much more likely to be aware of the child who is starting to become disaffected with school than is his subject–teacher colleague in a secondary school. The primary school teacher is also more likely to be aware of stressful situations in a child's family system and to judge whether the child has the skills to match the demands from home — let alone the demands from school. If the vulnerable child in his early years can be helped by his teacher to feel valued as a person and to maximise his educational potential this can provide him with a set of positive and rewarding constructs about attending school.

When a child has been forced to be absent through a serious illness or hospitalisation, he will have missed much of the work his peer group have learnt and therefore it is vitally important that time is given to him individually to help him to 'catch up'. Parents are usually only too happy to help their child if they are asked to assist the teacher in supervising extra work at home. Effects of enforced absence are then minimised and a pattern of absence through fear of academic failure and humiliation in the classroom situation need never be established.

Transfer from the warm, small, 'maternal' environment of primary school to the cold, large, impersonal environment of many secondary schools can be a stressful experience for many children but, with adequate support from family and the shared experience within a child's peer group, most children make the adjustment and find the new breadth of curriculum an exhilarating challenge. For the reasons already discussed, however, children who struggle academically, or come from homes where there are serious worries over money or relationships, or where they experience very little parental support, all find it much harder to make the adjustment. Reid (1986) condemns the way in which academic/pastoral dichotomies in many secondary schools have been fostered by prevailing career structures. The pastoral functions and responsibilities of heads of year differ greatly from the academic responsibilities of heads of department. A child who is experiencing emotional and behavioural difficulties which could lead to truancy will be viewed and treated inconsistently within such a dichotomous situation.

Where the pastoral system is not viewed as competitive with the academic system but is a highly valued element in a whole shool approach, priority will be given to swift follow-up of absence which is unsatisfactorily accounted for. Scrutiny of absence notes, communicating with parents and making a record of action taken at each stage, will become a matter of course.

To offer appropriate counselling to the child who truants requires his presence but, if he is secure in the knowledge that his pastoral mentor will treat him with respect and confidentiality, the truant may find in school exactly the form of emotional support which may be missing from his life.

Use of other agencies and resources

Galloway (1986) suggests that enlisting the help of an educational psychologist may be effective in some cases of truancy — especially if the pupil is pre-adolescent, treatment is provided soon after the onset of the problem and the school is actively involved. He also suggests that transfer to another school, including a move to a special school if appropriate, can, in selected cases, be beneficial.

The role of the educational welfare officer is well documented in the booklet *Attendance at School* published by the DES. Their duties include specific casework in identifying and following up pupils whose attendance is beginning to cause concern; working with primary and secondary school staff to facilitate transfer and visiting 'new' children's homes to introduce the school; the establishment of multi-disciplinary meetings to promote preventive action from agencies helping schools; running groups for potential long-term absentees and for their parents. The HMI who compiled the booklet found that the most effective form of support for the educational welfare service existed where the school and the EWOs shared clearly-defined criteria and procedures for referring non-attenders; the climate within the school was such that the perceptions of teachers and the EWOs about individual children and families were mutually informative and where preventive work within the school was the priority for both teachers and EWOs.

Conclusion

An examination of the child who becomes a persistent truant has revealed a complex relationship between factors in the child himself, his family and cultural background and, not least, factors within the school. Treatment of the individual child from a teacher's point of view should be a last resort. Preventive measures within schools involving an effective pastoral care system, an interesting and relevant curriculum and a whole school approach, which helps each child to feel valuable and valued, are likely to produce less long-term disaffection with school and to prevent truancy from becoming established as a 'norm' for some children. The support and co-operation of a trusted education welfare service and close, positive contact with the families of truants, who may be experiencing a specific or a multiplicity of personal, social and economic difficulties, is also likely to help to shut the gate *before* the horse has bolted. The Swann Report (DES, 1985) urged that all schools should develop a pattern of education which would enable all pupils to achieve their potential. This sentiment, intended for the education of ethnic minorities, would appear to be equally applicable to all children, including the truant.

CHAPTER SIX

EBD Associated with Physical Symptoms and Conditions

Introduction

In essence every form of illness to which human beings are subject has its psychosomatic aspects.

In fact the essential link between psychiatry and medicine lies in the ultimate difficulty in treating states of mind separately from states of body and states of body apart from states of mind.

We instinctively, when dealing with a child who has hurt himself and is suffering physical pain, give him warm hugs, gentle words and emotional comfort. Similarly, when we know a child to be suffering emotionally, we will offer him physical comfort in the form of warm holding, food and drinks that he likes.

A mutual interaction between emotional and physiological processes can be observed to be permanently in every human being whether he is perceived as functioning 'normally' or whether he is deemed to be suffering from an emotional and/or behavioural disturbance. Why then do we use the term 'psychosomatic' to imply that, in some way, the physical symptoms described by certain pupils are products of their imaginations?

In this chapter the relationship between psyche and soma, mind and body, will be examined in relation to the functions of breathing, eating, sleeping and elimination. Other observable emotional effects of problems associated with the body/brain specific learning difficulties, hyperactivity/attention deficit disorders and the effects of drug and solvent abuse will also be discussed.

Psychosomatic disorders

A psychosomatic disorder is the generic term used to describe either the physical effects of psychological disorders or the psychological effects of physical disorders. It is often difficult to determine which came first. For example, fear of leaving mother, in a school phobic child, can produce real stomach pains, nausea or vomiting. However, the child might have found that, early in his school career, when he was suffering from a genuine 'tummy upset', he was allowed to stay at home. Was his consequent 'sickness' at school time a piece of learnt behaviour reinforced by mother, who continued to let him miss school, and something which he could produce apparently at will; or was the emotional fear of separation from mother so strong that the physical response was out of his control?

The whole subject is, understandably, surrounded by controversy and there has been much debate as to which disorder, if any, should be considered under this heading. Views regarding the *concept* of psychosomatic disorders are changing. Lipowski (1984) proposes a holistic view in which all disorders, whether traditionally considered to be psychosomatic or not, are seen to involve the interplay of genetic predisposition, personality and environmental factors. The final symptom pattern produced by this interplay may then become a learned response. For example, high goal setting is stressful to some children, therefore, given a constitutional predisposition to asthma, a particular child with a high goal-setting mother or teacher may learn to have asthmatic attacks as an avoidance response to stress.

It is within this broad theoretical framework that emotional and behavioural problems which become apparent through physical symptoms will be discussed.

Childhood asthma

Melamed and Johnson (1981) found that asthma affects between two per cent and four per cent of children and that 60 per cent of all asthmatics are below the age of 17. Although the incidence is quite low it is likely that at some point in his career a teacher will have to deal with an asthmatic pupil. To witness a severe asthmatic attack can be very distressing as the child has severe difficulty in breathing, resulting from a narrowing of the air passages, usually due to increased mucus secretion. As an asthma attack can be potentially life-threatening, the teacher needs to know exactly what to do when responsible for an asthmatic child in terms of immediate medication.

The specific aetiology of asthma is uncertain but is now generally agreed to result from a complex interaction of genetically inherited allergies to specific substances such as a food, dust, a bird or an animal, together with psychological stimuli (Clemow,1984).

The emotional and behavioural disturbances which a child can be observed to be suffering as a result of being an asthmatic may show themselves in school through the child's perception of himself as *different*. The child may pity himself, restrict himself from some activities unnecessarily and keep himself apart from other children. The fear, misery and self-consciousness he experiences during an attack will be painful not only to him but also to his peers and teachers. His embarrassment may be exacerbated by overly solicitous parents who insist on 'showing him up' at school. At home his asthma may be the focus of attention from the whole family and the child may therefore become very attention-seeking at school.

Often both academic and social development suffer greatly because of the time lost at school and the teacher may be called upon to help the asthmatic child catch up by giving him extra teaching. Unfortunately, the asthmatic child can learn to manipulate others with the disorder or use it to avoid unpleasant activities or situations. Knowing when this is the case is difficult for the classroom teacher to weigh up and, understandably, we prefer to err on the side of caution.

Clear medical instruction as to the nature of drug treatment the child takes and knowledge of the steps to take when a child has an attack in class are essential. It is also going to help the child if the teacher can remain calm and perhaps seek assistance from a colleague to manage the rest of the class.

As family variables (Purcell, 1969) have been shown to be much more involved in the psychological element in asthma than school variables, the teacher's role is likely to be one of support for the child and co-operation with the parents.

Children who suffer from asthma are not an homogenous group. Unless the teacher is reasonably certain as to whether the child has asthma attacks in response to pressure from home — for instance, unrealistic goal-setting — or as a learned piece of behaviour to avoid doing something he regards as being unpleasant, it is difficult to know the most constructive approach to take. Discussion with the child and the family may help to confirm one hypothesis or the other but the first task is to provide the right medical treatment, usually a prescribed corticosteroid drug, and to help the child to cope with the panic and fear which almost inevitably accompany an attack. If the rest of the class have been informed and have discussed the child's condition prior to any attack in school, they will be able to provide emotional support and maintain a calm atmosphere conducive to reducing panic. Above all, the teacher should try to reduce the emotional stress in the child, both during an attack and in relation to school work he may have missed through enforced absence or hospitalisation.

Certain forms of brain injury may damage brain cells causing convulsions which vary from very bad (*grand mal*) to much milder (*petit mal*). A child experiencing a grand mal loses consciousness and the muscles contract violently. He may fall to the ground and lose bladder and bowel control and will jerk and twist before lapsing into a coma. The coma can last an hour or more and may be followed by headache and amnesia. Petit mal seizures last only a few seconds and may just appear to the teacher as short lapses in attention accompanied by muscular twitching.

As with childhood asthma, although the incidence is fairly low — Lubar and Shouse (1977) report only one in 250 — the onset is usually in childhood and a teacher is likely, in the course of his career, to come across at least one child who suffers from epilepsy. Although epilepsy is not truly a form of EBD and is usually well controlled with drug treatment, when a seizure does take place it is traumatic for the onlooker as well as for the child. Anxiety about having a seizure and resentment about being 'different' and 'odd' will certainly affect the child's self-perception.

As emotional stress can be one of the triggers for an epileptic seizure, the teacher will strive, as with the asthmatic child, to reduce unnecessary anxiety for the epileptic pupil. When an attack occurs the teacher should stay calm, put the child in the recovery position on his side, making sure that his air passage is free. The teacher can then turn his attention to the child's peers to reassure them and to enlist their support.

A brief discussion of epilepsy has been included in this section, rather than under EBD and Brain Pathology because, as with the asthmatic child, sometimes the trigger for an epileptic fit can be emotional. The author, for example, when headteacher of a school for EBD pupils, knew one epileptic girl who experienced a grand mal every time she was due to visit home. Within mainstream education an epileptic pupil may dread one teacher and this may be so stressful that seizures coincide with lessons with that teacher.

If an epileptic attack takes place in school the teacher's role is to provide the right medical and physical support but also to be aware of the trauma for the child and to try to minimise this by being understanding and supportive. The peer group, once it understands the condition, can also provide empathy and support.

Eating problems

Eating is the foremost activity of babies when they are awake and very early in life eating and food become associated with emotional security and love. In all cultures the offering and taking of food, or the deprivation of food, have strong emotional and psychological undertones, as well as constituting the governing factor between life and death and good and poor physical health.

Some disturbances of eating are only serious because they are potential sources of stress between mother and child, child and teacher, child and other adults in authority. For example, one of the earliest eating disorders, colic, usually found in infants up to five months old, can cause such anxiety, tension and ambivalence in the infant's mother, who is distressed by her baby's obvious pain but feels inadequate to deal with it, that her relationship with her child becomes one of guilt, frustration and fatigue. This tension and ambivalence can come to dominate both the mother's and the growing child's attitude to food, so that by the time he goes to school it is causing a real emotional and behavioural problem.

With the change to a cafeteria system within many school meal services, the teacher may have no idea whatsoever as to whether individual children are even eating adequately, let alone whether their attitude to food is a sign of emotional disturbance or friction at home. When school meals are closely supervised by staff, policies regarding how much persuasion/coercion should be used in encouraging a child to try a little of everything and to eat everything up, vary considerably. If a child is 'fussy' about his food is this because he has never been 'taught' to eat a balanced diet or is he in some way making an emotional protest or giving a cry for help?

Some children who have been deprived emotionally from early childhood can become obsessive eaters and start to add obesity to their many other problems. Their demand feeding is symbolic of their need for a steady supply of 'unconditional love and positive regard' (Rogers, 1957), from the adults close to them, including teachers, and yet the health hazard as well as the psychological ignominy of their 'fatness' cannot be ignored.

One is reminded of the little fat boy 'Piggy' in Golding's *Lord of the Flies*, who was continuously the butt of his peer group's wit and cruelty. Where a teacher knows that the child has suffered a great deal of rejection and emotional deprivation, tempting him to eat a more balanced and slimming diet needs to be paired with an attempt to meet his underlying emotional needs. There could, for example, be a high status, special slimmers' dining table or area where the child can share his sensible school meal with a teacher who is also trying to diet and can empathise with him. A system of rewarding a child with non-edible rewards such as extra time on his favourite activity when he refrains from overeating can be organised. If the child is a compulsive sweet and chocolate eater he could be offered a token for every half an hour he manages to pass without eating a sweet. These tokens could then be traded in later for an agreed reward.

For many children overeating is a learned piece of behaviour when either the mother has a psychological need to be feeding her child continuously, or she models obesity by overeating herself. If the teacher is to help this child to change his eating habits and to lose weight, which is causing him social stigma and therefore emotional disturbance, he will almost certainly have to gain the co-operation of the parents, especially the mother, and colleague members of staff.

Anorexia nervosa

One of the most serious eating problems to affect children, usually over the age of ten, is anorexia nervosa and its sister problem bulimia. Anorexia is characterised by peculiar attitudes towards eating and weight. This leads to an obsessive refusal to eat and consequently to profound weight loss. When it occurs in girls, and less than one in ten anorexics are boys, there is also persistent amenorrhoea, i.e. cessation of menstrual periods. It is an emotional and behavioural disorder which provides dramatic and very disturbing physical and life-threatening symptoms. In a school setting where meals are not supervised, teachers may be unaware that a child is becoming anorexic as the assumption will be that, if she appears to eat little to nothing at school, she is eating normally at home. The author was told recently of a girl whose mother thought she was eating at school and where the school thought she was eating at home, when in fact the girl had become severely anorexic. It was not until her appearance was positively skeletal that her disturbance was diagnosed.

Another factor which disguises the condition in some pupils is that they appear to eat normally, to 'binge' in fact, but then induce vomiting or take large quantities of laxatives to maintain their severe weight loss (i.e. they become bulimic).

In spite of their low calorific intake many anorexics are hyper-active and this again can mask the problem.

Halmi (1985) found that the peak age for onset was between 15 and 18 and therefore it is secondary school teachers who are most likely to come into contact with this form of EBD. There is also a link between anorexia and high intelligence and social class. Dally (1969) found that 90 per cent of a sample of anorexics had an IQ of 120+ and the majority were from middle and upper social classes.

At present, theories concerning the aetiology of anorexia are varied and confused. They range from those concerned with family variables, for example Minuchin (1974), who takes a systems approach to the problem, to Palmer (1980), who takes a biological approach and links anorexia with a malfunction of the hypoth-alamus.

From a teachers's point of view, theories which highlight the anorexic pupil's psychological fears are the most useful, as it is in this area that imaginative use of social and personal education within the curriculum may be of value. Crisp (1980), amongst other psycho-dynamically oriented researchers, views the latent anorexic as approaching puberty with fear, particularly of sexuality. The onset of adolescence means the end of childhood so the child regresses by giving up the outward signs of adolescence — in girls the develop-ment of breasts and the start of menstruation. More recently the onset of anorexia has been linked, in some cases, with a history of sexual abuse. Oppenheimer *et al* (1985) found that in a study of 78 latent anorexics 50 of the 78 had suffered sexual abuse in some form.

If frank and open discussion of puberty and adult sexuality and behaviour is part of the accepted content of sex education the pupil who has real or fantasy fears about sexual maturation may gain reassurance and support from teachers and peers. The physical problem of the dangerous loss of weight may mean a period of hospitalisation to ensure that the young person starts to eat but, once back at school, she or he will still need support, encouragement and counselling, as the low recovery rate of anorexics, between 40 per cent and 60 per cent (Crisp, 1977) and the high mortality rate, suggest a relatively poor prognosis.

Problems of sleep

Unless a teacher is employed in a boarding school problems to do with sleeping which a child is experiencing will be largely a matter of report by the parent or the child himself. Occasionally, however, a teacher will notice that a child appears to be very sleepy and tired in school and may choose to investigate the cause.

Problems to do with sleeping fall into two main categories:

- those involving failure to go to sleep
- those disrupting the continuity of sleep.

By and large children are rarely eager to go to bed and most young children invent lengthy bed-time rituals and ways of delaying bed-time which most parents collude with up to a reasonable point and then become firm.

If a child is described as having a serious problem in going to sleep it could be that this is a learned piece of behaviour, reinforced by over-collusive parents; or it could be a sign of intra-psychic conflicts. Bettelheim (1955), when writing about his work with emotionally disturbed children, reminds us that in sleep we are closest to our unconscious and that, if children have suffered traumatic experiences, these are likely to surface at bed-times.

If we know, from a child's history, that there are good reasons for him to be emotionally disturbed in a way which seriously affects his sleep we may, in school, be able to help him surface these conflicts and start to come to terms with them. In young children this could be through play; in older children through the use of art, music, drama or counselling sessions. The freedom to discuss dreams and nightmares and to find that teachers and peers also have frightening experiences during sleep at times can itself be reassuring.

Once again it is the relaxed, open and caring ethos of a school which will enable the emotionally disturbed pupil to perceive school as a place where he may seek reassurance and discuss personal problems. For some children it is the home environment which is inhibiting and he may feel ashamed of discussing there what seem to be irrational fears.

Problems of elimination

Control of the bowel and bladder have usually been achieved by the time a child who does not have severe learning or physical difficulties starts full-time education. Enuresis (lack of bladder control) and encopresis (lack of bowel control) in school age children are sometimes signs of emotional and behavioural disturbance and, because of their unpleasant nature, are unlikely to go unnoticed.

Even more than the problems of eating and sleeping, failures in toilet training are likely to upset parents and increase the probability of parent-child conflict. Damage to the child's self-esteem and problems of social adjustment, both at home and at school, are then inevitable.

The problem of enuresis appears to be a common one, particularly nocturnal enuresis. Christopherson and Rapoff (1983) suggest that as many as 20 per cent of all five-year olds and 10 per cent of all ten-year olds still wet the bed. Many of these children, however, will not be suffering from EBD. Either the child's ability to control the appropriate muscles is late in developing or he has not been taught at the appropriate age and stage to develop necessary conditioned reflexes.

If the child has been successfully 'potty trained' but then starts to wet the bed it is more likely that there is some emotional disturbance involved. Whereas many children who bed-wet are not emotionally disturbed, many children who are disturbed do in fact suffer from enuresis.

The extent to which nocturnal enuresis becomes a problem for the child at school is largely a question of social background. If the child is bathed every morning and has clean clothes, no-one at school may be aware of his problem. On the other hand, if the child has no opportunity to bath or shower he is likely to arrive at school smelly and highly noticeable.

The pastoral system within school may be limited in what it can offer to a child in this predicament and this is aggravated even further if the child wets in the day as well. Most schools would, in cases like this, refer the child to the school psychological services who would advise parents over direct treatment of the problem. This could take the form of behavioural treatment through the use of the bell and pad procedure, originally developed by Mowrer and Mowrer (1938); retention control training combined with positive reinforcement when the bed is dry. Alternatively, psychotherapy or family therapy might be offered.

The teacher's role is to protect the enuretic child from social isolation at school and, if the condition is a response to an upsetting event such as the birth of a sibling, mother going to hospital or a family death, to provide emotional support and comfort.

Encopresis (involuntary defecation not directly caused by physical disease), unlike enuresis, which is primarily nocturnal, usually takes place during the day and is even more distressing to both the child and those in close contact with him. Fortunately the incidence of encopresis in school age children is low; Doleys (1983) has cited figures as low as one per cent for children over ten years of age. Possible causes range from the behavioural to the psychoanalytic but advice to teachers would be the same as when dealing with enuresis – seek professional help and provide the least stressful environment for the child at school.

EBD and brain pathology

Many influences in a child's pre-natal and post-natal environment *may* give rise to neurological impairment, e.g. accidents in the birth process; maternal illness, for instance rubella during pregnancy; maternal stress; prematurity and low birth weight. If brain damage occurs later in the child's life he may have already developed some cognitive and social skills and it is sometimes difficult to determine the extent to which emotional and behavioural difficulties are a direct result of the brain damage or may be attributable to disturbing events or situations. A brain-damaged child who appears very anxious at school may be showing the effects of brain damage or he may be reacting to a difficult situation at home or within his peer group at school.

It is not the purpose of this chapter to look at brain pathology *per se* or to consider the emotional and behavioural difficulties of children with severe learning difficulties, but teachers wishing to further their understanding in this area are advised to start with the excellent study by Zarkowska and Clements (1988) *Problem Behaviour in People with Severe Learning Difficulties*.

There are certain conditions that may be perceived by teachers of children with low average to high intelligence to be indicative of EBD in which some form of brain damage has been hypothesised as *one* possible cause. Two of these, dyslexia/specific learning difficulties and hyperactivity/attention deficit disorder will now be discussed from the point of view of the emotional and behavioural difficulties which usually accompany them.

Dyslexia/specific learning difficulties

The term **dyslexia** used by the World Federation of Neurologists (1968) to define a disorder in children who, despite conventional classroom experience, fail to attain the language skills of reading, writing and spelling commensurate with their intellectual abilities, has been replaced by some psychologists and educationists more recently with the term **specific learning difficulties**. Tansley and Panckhurst (1981) who, amongst many others, prefer this term, state that children with specific learning difficulties are those who, in the absence of sensory defect or overt organic damage, have an intractable learning problem in one or more of reading, writing, spelling and mathematics, and who do not respond to normal teaching.

Whichever terminology we prefer the fact that these children have *learning* difficulties is not in dispute. Whether a child is suffering from *acquired dyslexia* as a result of specific brain damage or *specific developmental dyslexia*, where there is no history of trauma, he is likely to suffer emotionally from the stigma of being thought, quite wrongly, to be either stupid or lazy. Miles (1983) quotes the example of a boy whose mother wrote, 'he has been described in all school reports as "lazy", however he is very willing and helpful. He feels inadequate and resorts to irresponsible and anti-social behaviour to impress'.

Unless the specific learning difficulty has been diagnosed early in the child's school career he is likely to be labelled as EBD and treated accordingly, with secondary reference to his learning difficulties.

Awareness within the teaching profession of the existence of specific learning difficulty is, fortunately, increasing rapidly. Roughly half of the LEAs who responded in a recent survey (Cornwall, Hedderley and Pumfrey, 1984) state that they have policies to deal with specific reading difficulties. Screening at age seven is strongly recommended and teachers are encouraged to learn to recognise the warning signs. These signs are listed as: extreme and persisting difficulty in remembering and dealing with sequences, such as letters in written words; the sounds of oral words; sequences of numbers; problems with the recognition or retention of patterns; spelling errors which are particularly bizarre, unusual or distorted and may be marked by systematic errors with letter sequence, such as reversals, e.g. 'd' for 'b'.

A growing gap between a child's level of 'conceptual' understanding and his oral, writing, spelling and reading skills, are all indicative of possible specific reading difficulties. Although the incidence of specific reading difficulty is relatively low, Clark (1971) put the figure at one per cent of the average to the above average IQ population and the Dyslexia Society puts the figure at four per cent.

Arguments as to the aetiology of specific learning difficulties, or as they are commonly called, SLD, abound. Genetic factors, maturational lags, neurological dysfunction and cerebral dominance are all proposed as possible causes (Newton *et al.*, 1979).

Whatever the aetiology, the substantial overlap between specific learning difficulties and anti-social disorder noted by Rutter *et al.* (1970), which shows itself in restlessness, mischief making and poor relationships with other children, will inevitably cause the child to be regarded as EBD as well as stupid. The teacher may also find this child to be poorly motivated to learn and to appear to spurn any remedial teaching, especially if he has not been classified as 'dyslexic' until late in his school career. Repeated and misunderstood failure to learn has, understandably, diminished his motivation. Remediation of the emotional and behavioural disturbance is unlikely, therefore, to be achieved until the learning difficulty has been diagnosed, understood and specific, appropriate, remedial teaching initiated.

One of the factors that has helped the 'image' of dyslexia in recent times has been the 'coming out' of several successful people in the public eye, such as the actress Susan Hampshire who has modelled the fact that to be dyslexic/SLD can be overcome as a handicap.

The other very positive discovery recently has been that the use of a word processor can help to eliminate the SLD child's problems with writing and spelling. In an article in the *Times Educational Supplement*, (8 March 91), Paris Innes, a 14-year old dyslexic, describes how through sheer frustration and despair about his learning difficulty at age 12 he packed his bags and left home. From early days in school his mother had worried about him and all his unrecognised class symptoms of SLD – confusion of letters, left and right, clock faces, columns of numbers, word spelling and pen manipulation. Accompanying these were his psychological problems — truanting, low self-esteem, hypersensitivity. A family friend and doctor, who was also dyslexic, suggested that Paris used a typewriter and this in turn led to him using a word processor. Paris has now published his first novel.

Quite clearly, the first step for the teacher is to have an early diagnosis of the learning problem, and to achieve this the assistance of the educational psychologist will be invaluable. A specialist support teacher will also be desirable, where resources allow, but above all, from the point of view of the child's emotional and behavioural difficulties, the teacher who is armed with the correct diagnosis of and prescription for the learning difficulty will now see the child's anti-social behaviour as an expression of a real need for acceptance, understanding and help.

Hyperactivity/attention deficit disorder

This form of EBD was originally called Strauss syndrome after A. A. Strauss, who associated the condition solely with brain damage. The children involved are not an homogenous group and many children who could be classified as **hyperactive** show no sign of brain damage.

When the term hyperactive was replaced by the term **attention deficit disorder** in the *Diagnostic and Statistical Manual of Mental Disorders* (DSM 111, 1980, American Psychiatric Association), this was an acknowledgement of the fact that the child's problem, particularly in a school setting, was frequently as much to do with his inability to concentrate for any length of time, as with his level of activity. The DSM 111 gave the following criteria for the diagnosis of attention deficit with hyperactivity:

A. INATTENTION At least three of the following:
(1) Often fails to finish things he or she starts
(2) Often doesn't seem to listen
(3) Easily distracted
(4) Has difficulty concentrating on schoolwork or other tasks requiring sustained attention
(5) Has difficulty sticking to a play activity

B. IMPULSIVITY At least three of the following:
(1) Often acts before thinking
(2) Shifts excessively from one activity to another
(3) Has difficulty organising work (this not being due to cognitive impairment)
(4) Needs a lot of supervision
(5) Frequently calls out in class
(6) Has difficulty awaiting turn in games or group situations

C. HYPERACTIVITY At least two of the following:
(1) Excessively runs about or climbs on things
(2) Has difficulty sitting still or fidgets excessively

(3) Has difficulty staying seated
(4) Moves about excessively during sleep
(5) Is always 'on the go' or acts as if 'driven by a motor'

D. ONSET before the age of seven.

E. DURATION of at least six months.

F. NOT DUE to schizophrenia, affective disorder, or severe or profound mental retardation.

Theories of aetiology range from minimal brain damage to vitamin deficiency and, as the group is not homogenous, research has produced results to support a number of hypotheses. David (1974) found that hyperactive children with no known organic aetiology had significantly higher levels of lead in their blood streams than children in a control group. This had been caused by chewing paint on toys or furniture and, more recently, from car fumes. Crook (1980) maintained that food allergies could cause hyperactivity and Feingold (1968) established that the use of dyes in foods could also be responsible. In a review of genetic studies, McMahon (1980) found a higher incidence of hyperactivity in the relatives of hyperactive children than in the population generally or in families where the child was adopted.

From the teacher's point of view, whatever the aetiology, the hyperactive child with ADD will not go unnoticed at school! The child's restlessness, attention seeking behaviour, difficulty in concentration and ability to irritate other children proclaim him as suffering from behavioural disturbance if not emotional disorder.

Studies by Loney (1983) suggest that there are two major sub-types of attention deficit disorder:

(1) An aggressive type of attention disorder in which the child has many interpersonal difficulties.
(2) A non-aggressive type of attention deficit disorder in which poor academic performance is the major problem.

Zentall (1975) proposed a further sub-type in which ADD children with hyperactivity have a lower than optimal state of arousal and engage in frantic extra activity in order to increase their level of stimulation.

The teacher faced with coping with and attempting to teach an ADD child with hyperactivity will need to form a hypothesis then test it as to which of these three sub-categories the pupil can be ascribed.

The aggressive hyperactive child with many interpersonal difficulties may be acting out in the school environment aggression and frustration which he is experiencing at home. He may, for example, be the victim of physical, emotional or sexual abuse at home. He may be completely rejected by one or both parents or be the scape-goat member of the family. Where knowledge of the family background proves this hypothesis to be correct, the teacher will try to refrain from reinforcing the child's feeling of unworthiness and low self-esteem and will try to reduce the hyperactivity, (a) by giving the child the opportunity to discuss, or play out, the internal conflict; and (b) by giving positive rewards every time the child controls his anti-social, over-active behaviour and concentrates for increasingly greater lengths of time.

If the teacher forms the hypothesis that a particular child with ADD and hyperactivity has general or specific learning difficulties of which the hyperactivity is a by-product his approach will be educational. In order to help the child sit still long enough to be given remedial education a programme of behaviour modification through positive reinforcement may again be employed. This child will also be suffering from low self-esteem but this will be raised considerably as he makes academic progress. If the services of a support teacher are available, for even a short period of time, this will prove invaluable.

There is a very small proportion of children, approximately one in 10,000, whose IQ is so above the norm for their age, that they may present as hyperactive at school because they are under stimulated academically. In a recent BBC television programme, *40 Minutes* (March 1991), several children in this category were interviewed and filmed at school. One little boy in particular who was six years old and had the IQ of a ten-year old was particularly restless, and his teacher admitted that it was difficult to provide him with work which was challenging enough. Another nine-year old complained that the teacher didn't like 'brainy boys' because they did all the work too quickly! He said that cleverness seemed to be viewed as an illness and, in fact, he had been suffering severely from nightmares. Pupils like this may not appear often in a teacher's life but when they do they are not straightforward to teach and assistance may well be needed.

The hypothesis proposed by Zentall (1975) that ADD children find difficulty in being aroused and should therefore be surrounded by a highly stimulating environment was a direct antithesis of one traditional view of hyperactivity, based on the assumptions of Strauss, and in which he maintained that hyperactive children are brain damaged and unable to 'screen out' incoming stimuli. In this model, hyperactivity is a result of overstimulation so the teacher should strive to provide a classroom, or at least an area, as devoid of stimulation as possible. Windows should be opaque, walls, floors and ceilings should be painted the same colour and there should be no pictures or excess furniture (Cruikshank, 1961). These latter recommendations could only be carried out in a highly specialised educational setting and studies comparing hyperactive children assigned to normal and stimulus-reduced environments have been inconclusive (Zentall, 1975).

ADD with hyperactivity is not an unusual problem for the classroom teacher to encounter in one form or another. Some studies e.g. Whalen and Henker (1980), go as high as 20 per cent with the sex ratio varying from 3:1 to 9:1 in favour of boys.

Attempts to diagnose the causes of the problem should be made with the assistance of medical and psychological services. Methods of intervention will need similarly to be worked out in conjunction with professional psychological help.

For many classroom teachers behavioural approaches to the classroom management of hyperactive children have proved most productive, but where an emotional disturbance is thought to underlie the ADD behaviour some form of therapy, individual or family, might be recommended outside school (Wheldall, 1987).

Drug abuse

The abuse of drugs, including tobacco and alcohol, is becoming an increasing problem within our society and this is reflected, not surprisingly, at school level. Although the abuse of drugs by children is not as prevalent in Britain as one is led to believe it is in the United States, teachers and parents are nevertheless anxious that it should not become so.

Is dependency on drugs a form of EBD or is it a result of EBD? These are questions to which there are no pat answers but, as members of a profession which aims to educate the 'whole child', we cannot turn a blind eye. If the teacher is aware of the warning signals and has enough knowledge about the facts surrounding the subject, he is in a better position to intervene constructively when a child presents as EBD, as a result of drug abuse.

Johnston *et al.* (1981) report that alcohol and cigarettes are the most widely used drugs amongst adolescents but that up to 17 per cent of adolescents have used, at least once, marijuana, stimulants, inhalants, cocaine, sedatives, hallucinogens, tranquillisers and other opiates. As more than 90 per cent of secondary school pupils have used alcohol at some time and 70 per cent have smoked cigarettes (Johnston *et al.*, 1981) these are drug users with whom *every* secondary school teacher is going to come into contact.

The Health Education Authority, on finding that eight per cent of nine-year olds have tried smoking and that by the age of 11 that figure has doubled, has stressed the need for teachers to start, at primary level, an education programme which will not only teach children how their bodies function but also point out the dangers of smoking. The 'My Body' project based at the Southfield Curriculum and Professional Development Centre, Gleadless Road, Sheffield, has been adapted to fit in with key stage 2 of the National Curriculum (for children aged seven to 11). It aims to give children decision-making skills so that they can decide whether to smoke or not.

From personal experience as a headteacher I know it is very difficult to impose a ban at secondary school level on cigarettes and alcohol which can truly be enforced. By all means ban smoking in areas which are regularly supervised but too much emphasis on rules which are impossible to enforce can rebound on the staff. Smoking and drinking alcohol are portrayed in the mass media and perceived by some adolescents as signs of being a successful, sophisticated adult. To a young person seeking adult status these activities can constitute a powerful model of being 'grown up'.

The use of imaginative social and personal education programmes which involve the pupils in an enjoyable way are far more likely to have long reaching effects than a Draconian system of rules and punishments. At Grangemouth High School in Scotland an anti-smoking project was designed by staff and pupils together, in which pupils produced rap lyrics and enlisted the support of a popular Glasgow Rangers football player to help make an anti-smoking video. Similar projects could be designed to illustrate the dangers and discuss the use of alcohol as a drug.

Perhaps it should be added that these innovative approaches are more likely to succeed if the staff can resist modelling the habits they are striving to discourage in the pupils!

The Research of Kandel (1982) indicates that children who become dependent on drugs pass through a developmental progression of different levels towards more and more serious drug involvement. An adolescent is likely to begin by using beer and wine, followed by spirits and/or cigarettes, then on to marijuana and finally to other illicit drugs.

Unfortunately there are now many illicit drugs available to young people and, depending on the particular population of the school, teachers will come into contact with pupils who may be using them. It is probably valuable, therefore, to be acquainted with some of the street jargon that relates to such substances:

OPIODS Heroin, Morphine, Chasing the Dragon, Smack, H, Stuff, Junk.

STIMULANTS Speed (amphetamine); Sulph (amphetamine sulphate); Pep Pills (stimulants); Blues, Bluies (blue amphetamine pills); Coke (cocaine); Uppers (stimulants); Toppers; Kickers.

SEDATIVES Barbs (barbiturates); Nembies (Nembutal); Seckies (seconal); Libs, Green and Blacks (Librium); Downers, Sleepers (depressants); Red Chicken (heroin on a barbiturate base); Vals (valium); Valium cocktails (valium mixed with alcohol).

PSYCHEDELICS Dots (microdots, LSD); Acid, a tab of acid (LSD); STP (serenity, tranquillity, peace); Mushrooms (usually Liberty Gap mushrooms); Sausage, THC, Resin (cannabis); Dope, Pot, Weed, Tea, Grass, Brownies (all marijuana); Ganja (West Indian hashish); Joint, Smoke (cannabis cigarettes); Seeds, Pearly Gates (morning glory seeds).

The effects of drugs can be termed: buz, hit, high, trip; and the effects of withdrawal: crashing out, cold turkey. Frightening hallucinations may be referred to as squealies.

Some of the signs and symptoms associated with specific drugs are as follows:

A. BARBITURATE ABUSER
   Drowsiness
   Staggering
   Lack of interest
   Appears disoriented
B. AMPHETAMINE ABUSER – STIMULANTS
   Pupils dilated, eyes prominent and staring
   Hyperactivity

Easily irritated
Dizziness
Accident prone
Loss of appetite
Weight loss
Erratic sleep patterns
C. MAGIC MUSHROOM ABUSE
Bizarre and very disturbing hallucinations
Disorientation
Increased heart beat
Feelings of persecution
Irrational fears
Appears to be in a dream-like state
Lapses into sleep/unconsciousness
Has bad trips (as in LSD effects)

The onlooker to a child who has become dependent on drugs may feel that there cannot be a single rational argument to support the child's behaviour. The habitual drug user, however, has a very different construct of the situation and if the teacher is to gain the pupil's confidence in order to help him to 'kick the habit' then he must first of all try to understand the child's construct of reality.

In many cultures throughout the world the use of drugs as a means of relaxing and 'getting into the party spirit' is socially quite acceptable. Children, therefore, grow up with models of drug abuse all around them. If, in addition to this, the children have stressful family situations, or have become accustomed to being made to feel worthless at home and/or school, the short-term positive effects of drug taking can well seem to out-weigh the long-term dangers. For the EBD child the three primary gains of taking drugs identified by O'Connor (1986) as 'excitation, relaxation and perceptual change' can provide temporary release from a hum-drum, bewildering or frightening life. Expressed in another way, the young drug user experiences gratification in ways which meet different personal and social needs and which can also be sequentially related. They are detailed as follows:

STAGE 1 Experimentation: drugs are used for fun and to satisfy curiosity or to experiment with feelings.
STAGE 2 Social-reactional: drugs are used to share a common experience with friends.

STAGE 3 Circumstantial – situational: drugs are used to help in coping with moods, work and sex.

STAGE 4 Intensified: drugs are used to escape from problems, including emotional problems.

STAGE 5 Compulsive: drugs are used to maintain a drug high or drugged state.

Concerned teachers will attempt to identify children who are at an early stage, especially children who have a history of EBD or are known to be in a situation which is likely to produce EBD. Rather like sex education, drug education should be an integral part of the life skill curriculum for *all* children and should not be kept in reserve until something tragic takes place.

Solvent abuse

Glue-sniffing is still identified as the popular name for solvent abuse but in fact 'solvents under abuse' now constitute a very wide range of substances which include hair-sprays, dry-cleaning fluids, felt-tip marker pens, petrol, body deodorants, metal polish, as well as many different types of adhesives. Although most known solvent abusers are boys, in the age range 12 to 17 years, Kandel suggests that this is because girls tend to be less obvious about the habit. Indications are, according to O'Connor (1986), that some three per cent to five per cent of 15-year olds have used solvents at some time. Some children become involved in sniffing out of curiosity and some children to maintain acceptance in their peer group. Many such children are not emotionally or behaviourally disturbed and soon give the practice up after initial experimentation. A study in Tyne and Wear (1983), however, revealed that at least 10 per cent of the young people who use solvents will develop a chronic problem. For these children the physical and psychological dependency on the albeit temporary feeling of intoxication, relaxation and well-being which sniffing brings is likely to be a substitute for real security and affection in their lives. The following example from the Newcastle University Counselling Clinic illustrates the point:

> I cannot help worrying about why my dad will have nothing to do with us now. I wonder where he is and why he left us. When I sniff glue it is like we are all back together again.

As this type of child from a disadvantaged background is unlikely to have much money to indulge his habit he invariably becomes involved in theft, usually with a group of fellow sniffers, in order to buy solvents.

The most serious short-term effects of solvent abuse can be hallucinations and possible collapse into a coma. The less dramatic effects involve slurring of speech, lack of co-ordination and blurring of vision — all of which can lead to accidents. The long-term effects will almost certainly involve lasting damage to the heart, kidneys and liver and, of course, lead even to death.

If a teacher can be aware of the risks at an early stage of a child's potential dependency on solvent abuse he may be able to intervene constructively before the habit becomes ingrained. Some of the signs to watch out for include: sores around the mouth and nostrils; chemical smells on the breath; traces of solvents on the type of equipment used for sniffing, e.g. plastic bags, crisp packets, milk bottles, lapels or sleeves; a fixed stare; sudden violent behaviour or unexpected mood swings. As with most forms of EBD, the teacher's relationship with the pupil will determine to what extent the underlying reasons for the need to escape into the 'other world' of drugs can be openly discussed. Counselling at this stage by the teacher or a colleague with specialised knowledge may prevent the problem from becoming acute.

If it is possible, without destroying the child's trust through breaking confidentiality, parents and helping agencies may be contacted to give support outside school hours. If there is a known group of solvent abusers in the school a teacher with pastoral/counselling responsibility may be able to organise group therapy sessions, either on his own initiative if suitably qualified, or with the assistance of specialist help from agencies such as the National Campaign Against Solvent Abuse (55 Wood Street, Mitcham Junction, Surrey). Once a child has become highly dependent on solvent abuse, the classroom teacher should not hesitate to consult with appropriate outside agencies as the child may be in need of hospital treatment or a course of therapeutic rehabilitation that lies outside the resources of the school.

Conclusion

In this chapter a broad review of psychological problems associated with physical symptoms has been undertaken. In some cases the physical condition from which the child suffers has been seen to give rise to psychological stress, e.g. asthma. In other cases the underlying psychological need has been seen to give rise to physical symptoms, e.g. chronic drug abuse. The teacher who works in a special EBD school is likely to have come across examples of all the problems discussed and to be familiar with some of the strategies for dealing with them. Within mainstream education, especially where the academic needs of the pupils take high priority over the pastoral needs, some of these children may not be identified as having special emotional needs or there may not be the resources available to meet them. Sometimes though the need can be met at very little material cost if a teacher is sensitive to the distress signals which the child sends out. The teacher may then find that many of the upsetting physical manifestations of psychological distress (and the psychological manifestations of physical distress) in the child can be reduced to a minimum and not allowed to disrupt the normal harmonious tenor of the classroom day.

CHAPTER SEVEN

Psychoneurotic and Psychotic Disorders in Childhood

Introduction

All forms of EBD are related in some way to stress and a child's attempt, usually inappropriate or inadequate, to cope with anxiety. If we refer back (Chapter One) to the classifications of EBD proposed by Achenbach, Quay and Rutter, we find a group of children who internalise rather than externalise their problems and impose demands and inhibitions on themselves as opposed to acting out aggressively towards others. This internalisation of anxiety forms the common basis of specific disorders, the psychoneuroses of childhood, to be discussed in the first part of this chapter. In the second part of the chapter the most extreme form of EBD — psychosis in childhood — will be examined briefly.

The major difference between these two serious forms of emotional and behavioural disturbance is that, whilst the neurotic child is adapting, in an unhappy way, to his real life situation, the psychotic child is attempting to adapt to a subjectively distorted concept of himself and of the world around him.

1. NEUROTIC DISORDERS

The neurotic disorders of childhood are less severe than the psychotic disorders but are nevertheless highly disturbing to the child and should be disturbing to all those in contact with him, including teachers. They are not thought to be the result of organic causes and are invariably characterised by high levels of anxiety which interfere with the child's ability to function intellectually, socially and emotionally.

Psychologists like Eysenck (1947) suggested that constitutional factors may play a role in the development of neurotic disorders, especially in conjunction with environmental stress. Another factor that may influence the development of neurotic disorders in childhood is temperament (Dollinger, 1983). Some children from birth are more fearful of new experiences, often withdraw emotionally and are 'difficult' children.

The inherent danger for this type of child in a busy, hectic classroom and school is that, because he is internalising his anxieties and may be causing no 'overt' problem for teacher or peers, he will be overlooked and not perceived as having special needs. The author can recall one teen-age girl whose desperately unhappy neurotic approach to life had been totally unobserved until she made a very serious attempt at suicide.

Neurotic disorders in childhood will be discussed under the three general headings of:

- anxiety disorders
- somatoform disorders
- affective disorders.

Anxiety disorders

(a) Over-anxious disorder

We are all familiar with the pupil who never seems to stop worrying and often displays nervous habits such as nail-biting and hair pulling. These children find it very difficult to relax and need constant reassurance over a variety of worries from fear of the future to over concern about competence in a number of areas, e.g. academic, social, athletic. They feel very self- conscious, are easily embarrassed and may at times seem mature for their age because they worry about what we consider to be 'adult' matters. The author can recall one little seven-year old boy who was already worrying about who was going to pay his pension when he retired as there would be so many old people alive by then!

If it is purely a matter of temperament the teacher may be able to do very little to alleviate this child's anxiety but very often this innate propensity for worrying is being exacerbated by over demands and expectations of the child, both academically and socially, at home and at school. It is not just coincidence that over-anxious disorder is found more frequently in boys, amongst eldest children and in families where there are excessive demands for high levels of performance (Schwarz and Johnson, 1985).

The teacher can help the child to realise that performances at school which fall short of perfection are still highly acceptable and that it is good to relax for five minutes or so at the end of each lesson by, for example, taking it in turns to tell a joke to the class. The child's view of school may then gradually become less anxiety-provoking.

Since anxiety is a reflex reaction to the presence of danger it will be triggered off when a child is faced with an event or demand he feels he cannot handle. If we can take the time to discuss these triggering events with an over-anxious child and then, in discussion and co-operation with him, devise a plan which will give him the necessary skills to handle the threat, we can go a long way to reassure this 'wee timorous beastie' that there is not a catastrophe lurking just around every corner in life! Learning to relax by taking deep breaths when anxiety starts to mount can be a useful technique for this child to learn.

(b) Avoidant/separation disorders

It is natural for very young children to be afraid of strangers but after the age of about three and certainly by the time the child enters full-time education this shrinking from strangers has usually stopped.

At the age of development when a child starts to learn to be independent, to walk and to dress and feed himself, there may be a reluctance, albeit unconscious, on the part of one or both parents to see the child grow up and move away from the symbiotic closeness of the mother/baby relationship. The process of growing independence is then hampered. The child who suffers this form of deprivation may well develop severe anxiety over meeting strangers and/or separating from those to whom he is emotionally attached. These children refuse to go to school or anywhere without their parents and worry constantly about possible harm that might befall those close to them in their absence. They are also likely to develop physical symptoms such as headaches, nausea and vomiting if separation from parents or the need to interact socially with others is forced upon them.

Most infant teachers will have encountered children like this and are usually skilled at bridging the gap between mother and school but if this anxiety disorder persists into later childhood the problems for the child and the teacher are likely to be less manageable. As these children often appear excessively shy and timid but do not present control problems for the busy teacher they may not be perceived as having special educational needs and may be over-looked until for instance they have developed chronic school phobia.

Childhood fears and phobias

Fear can be a healthy, normal response to an objective source of danger and provide the correct response to deal with that danger – e.g. running away from fire. Fears are also a common problem of childhood and may be linked to developmental stages, in which case a child will usually outgrow them naturally. Miller (1983) lists what he terms stage-specific fears as follows:

Age	Fears
0 – 6 months	loud noises, loss of support
6 – 9 months	strangers
1st year	separation, injury, toilet
2nd year	imaginary creatures, death, robbers
3rd year	dogs, being alone
4th year	the dark
5th – 12th year	school, injury, natural events
13th – 18th year	injury, social fears
19th year +	injury, natural events, sexual

These 'normal' fears in childhood are usually overcome through reassurance and through adults and older siblings modelling lack of fear of the aversive stimulus. In order to bring into the open and come face to face with the natural fears and 'bogeymen' at each stage, and thereby to start to overcome irrational fears, the imaginative teacher can organise projects which incorporate them. We can all recall personally and through the children we teach the delight and horror combined in telling and listening to ghost stories at a certain developmental stage.

If fear becomes obsessive and does not resolve itself, or if it creates a serious problem for a child, preventing him from taking part in the experiences and activities appropriate to his age, it can be termed pathological. The child has become greatly pre-occupied with the feared stimulus or situation and his fearfulness is intense, frequent and persistent.

Miller *et al.* (1974) proposed that a phobia is a fear characterised by the following seven features:

(1) It is out of proportion to the demands of the situation.
(2) It cannot be explained or reasoned away.
(3) It is beyond voluntary control.
(4) It leads to avoidance of the feared situation.

(5) It persists over an extended period of time.
(6) It is unadaptive.
(7) It is not age specific.

There are four major categories of phobia identifiable in children:

FEAR OF PHYSICAL INJURY (e.g. abstract fears of war, dying, germs; and concrete fears such as flying in an aeroplane, high places, deep water].
FEAR OF NATURAL EVENTS (e.g. storms, the dark, enclosed places, spiders, snakes, dogs, space creatures or monsters, fire, sight of blood).
SOCIAL ANXIETIES (e.g. school, reciting in class, performance in tests or exams, separation from parents, crowds, doctors, dentists, travelling in buses or trains, and social interaction generally).
MISCELLANEOUS FEARS (e.g. dirt, furry toys, people in uniforms, people of another race).

If a teacher is aware that a pupil is suffering from a specific phobia he may be able to help that pupil to start to overcome the phobia by initiating a programme of systematic desensitisation. Ideally this would be undertaken in one to one counselling sessions and would fall within the realms of a teacher with a designated counselling/pastoral role in school. If there are no such resources available it would be possible to organise a class project in which all pupils would be involved but which is targeted at the particular phobia of the child concerned. Learning how to tackle, in a relatively simple but well planned way, something which causes unnecessary fear is a useful skill for any child to acquire and could legitimately be seen as a relevant component of the personal and social education syllabus.

Taking an imaginary case of a pupil who has a phobia about heights the programme of intervention could be planned as follows:

(1) The teacher, with the rest of the children, helps the child to construct an anxiety hierarchy or a ranked list of situations to do with heights. This might look something like:
    (a) Walking near the edge of a cliff and looking down
    (b) Standing on a hill looking down at a stream
    (c) Looking out of the window from the fifth floor
    (d) Walking down a long stairway
    (e) Standing on a stool and reaching for something
    (f) Standing still on a bench
    (g) Standing on a stage
    (h) Standing firmly on flat ground.

(2) The child, or group of children, is then taught how to relax. Ideally the setting for this intervention will be a room which is carpeted and comfortable with soft lighting and no fear of interference from outside. If this is not available the children may be able to sit comfortably on the floor of, say, the gymnasium. They are then asked firstly to tense up and then relax different muscles in turn (Lennox,1982), thus achieving maximum relaxation whilst the teacher talks soothingly to them, conjuring up relaxing images, such as lying on a beach in the sunshine.

(3) Once relaxation has been achieved, the teacher asks the child and, if undertaken in class, the whole group to visualise and imagine being in the situations described in the hierarchy — starting with the least threatening, e.g. standing firmly on the ground, and then on to the others progressively, though not all in the course of one lesson! It may well span three or four lessons.

(4) Once the child has conquered each situation and learnt to control his anxiety in conjunction with relaxing his body the teacher can go on to expose the child, in graduated steps, to the actual situations about which the child is phobic.

It is important that the process is not hurried and that each step should be preceded by a period of relaxation and paired with something the child finds pleasurable, such as holding the teacher's hand or eating a sweet.

To use the example of the child who has a phobia about heights, each step in the hierarchy of feared situations could quite easily be incorporated into a 'normal' school activity and the teacher could be engaged in a programme of systematic desensitisation with the phobic child without neglecting the other members of the class — indeed their co-operation could be actively enlisted.

For other more unusual phobias the child may have to be referred to an educational or clinical psychologist but, as teachers, if we have insight into the problem there is much that we can offer within our normal curriculum. A comprehensive guide to the understanding and treatment of fears and phobias in childhood is provided by Morris and Kratochwill (1983).

School phobia

The most common form of phobia that a teacher is likely to come across is school phobia or, as it is often termed, school refusal.

Whereas the truant, discussed in Chapter Five, is usually absent from school without the parents' knowledge and is deemed to be in the conduct disorder category of EBD, the child who suffers from school phobia is usually in the neurotic, anxiety withdrawn category of EBD. He or she is absent from school with the parents' knowledge and with implicit if not explicit approval.

Berg (1980), from his study of school phobic boys and girls admitted to a psychiatric in-patient unit, suggests the following criteria for the diagnosis of school phobia/school refusal:

(1) Severe difficulty in attending school usually amounting to prolonged absence.
(2) Severe emotional upset when faced with the prospect of going to school, including excessive fearfulness, undue tempers, misery and complaints of feeling ill, without an organic cause being found.
(3) Staying at home with the knowledge of their parents when they should be at school.
(4) Absence of significant anti-social disorders, such as stealing, lying, wandering, destructiveness.

The most common explanation for the refusal to go to school in school phobic children is not that they actually have a phobia about school but that they are suffering from acute separation anxiety. This predominantly psycho-analytic explanation also stresses the role of the mother whom Kelly (1973) found to be often mildly neurotic herself with unresolved dependency needs.

Anxiety about attending school, however, produces different subgroups, which have different implications for treatment. Yule, Hersov and Tresider (1980) propose the following sub-divisions:

(1) Children who show refusal to go to school from the start and this is probably a manifestation of separation anxiety, complicated by the mother's reluctance to part with her child.
(2) Children who are reluctant to go to school after the critical change from a small primary school to a large secondary school. The child may suddenly find that, having been the brightest pupil in the class, he now faces steep competition and the sheer size of many secondary schools can be overwhelming.
(3) Occasionally, where a child has formerly attended school regularly for many years, the onset of phobia may be due to the onset of a depressive illness or as a symptom of a deep emotional disturbance as in for example the sexually abused child.

(4) Enforced absence through illness may produce a reluctance to return to school because of fear of 'being behind' in classwork. If this is colluded with by a mother who 'prolongs' the child's illness and encourages the child to stay at home, this can become a learned piece of avoidance behaviour.

(5) Reluctance to go to school because of specific happenings there (e.g. being bullied, ridiculed) or handled insensitively when there has been a *real* trauma for the child (e.g. a bereavement at home).

Although the presenting behaviour is the same, refusal to come to school, the teacher will employ slightly different strategies in each of the above cases.

The infant and mother who show reluctance to part from each other could be encouraged to join a group of other parents who take part in school social and fund-raising events and in the process gain reassurance from them that going to school is a normal, non-threatening experience for the child and mother and that the school day in fact passes quite quickly.

The transition from primary to secondary school can be eased considerably by well planned liaison and co-operation between top junior feeder schools and the intake forms of the secondary school. Visits and parents' evenings can do much to allay anxiety and the interaction between 'new' parents and between 'new' pupils can be very reassuring.

If the reluctance to attend school appears to be linked to the onset of serious emotional difficulties the class teacher would be wise to consult with senior staff who will the refer the child to the appropriate agencies for more specialised help.

The child who has been absent through illness and then becomes a school refuser can be helped through, for instance, contingency contracting as described by Weathers and Liberman (1975). A written 'contract' is agreed upon with the co-operation of the pupil, his parents and teachers involved with him at school. This document specifies the desired behaviour — regular attendance at school — and the consequences that will follow when the desired behaviour does or does not occur. The parents, child, and teacher are all asked to state what they are prepared to give for what and a system of meaningful rewards is decided upon. This programme will almost inevitably include, as a reward, extra time on missed work from the teacher backed up by active co-operation from the parents. The contract is signed by all concerned, reviewed at regular intervals and dispensed with once regular attendance has been happily re-established.

For the child who is refusing school because of a specific fear of what happens to him at school, such as being bullied, it is sometimes difficult for the teacher to identify the cause. The nature of bullying, to be discussed more fully in Chapter Nine, is such that the victim is often too frightened to tell anyone and the problem can be masked by, say, illness as a way of avoiding confrontation and fear at school. The child may then come to exemplify the 'masquerade syndrome' described by Waller and Eisenberg (1980) in which 'week-day morning sickness' such as tummy-aches, vomiting or headaches are really experienced by the child, until he is declared too ill to go to school. Once school attendance has been ruled out that day the symptoms magically disappear! Unless the real cause of the child's fear can be identified and dealt with, treatment will tend to be cosmetic and its success short-lived. This emphasises once again the teacher's need to be aware of and to understand what is troubling a disturbed child.

Kennedy (1965) identified two major types of school phobia, stating that a diagnosis of school phobia is warranted in either type if seven of the ten characteristics listed should apply:

TYPE 1 Neurotic, acute school phobia
 (1) The present illness is the first episode.
 (2) The onset is on a Monday following an illness the previous Thursday or Friday.
 (3) The onset is acute.
 (4) The child is still young.
 (5) The child worries about death.
 (6) The mother is actually ill or the child thinks she is.
 (7) There is good communication between parents.
 (8) Mother and father are basically well adjusted.
 (9) Father is competitive with mother in managing the household.
(10) Parents are easy to work with.

TYPE 2 Characterological, chronic school phobia
 (1) There have been several episodes of 'illness'.
 (2) Monday onset following minor illness is not a usual antecedent.
 (3) The onset is gradual.
 (4) The child is older.
 (5) Death is not a particular worry.
 (6) Mother's health is not an issue.
 (7) The parents communicate poorly with each other.

(8) Mother is neurotic, father shows a character disorder.
(9) Father shows little interest in household management or the children.
(10) Both parents are difficult to work with.

The prognosis for Type 1 school phobic children, who are in the majority, is optimistic if given treatment — usually in the form of systematic desensitisation as previously described. The physical problems are ignored and the child is rewarded heavily for each step he takes towards conquering his fear.

For Type 2 school phobic children, who are fortunately rare, the prognosis is much more pessimistic. In the study quoted by Kennedy (1965) school phobia was only one of these children's difficulties and they came from families in which at least one parent was seriously disturbed.

Whilst it is extremely helpful to enlist the support of educational social workers, educational or clinical psychologists in developing strategies to help the Type 1 school phobic child, it is absolutely necessary to refer the school phobic Type 2 child for psychological/psychiatric help.

In the wake of the Education Reform Act schools are being urged to publish their attendance figures as predictors of the school's overall attractiveness to parents and indicators of all round competence. Knowledge not only of the child who truants persistently but also of the child who is suffering from neurotic anxiety leading to school phobia is therefore going to be vital.

Obsessions and compulsions

Most children display some form of minor obsessional behaviour at certain developmental stages. Believing that disaster will be inevitable if one treads on the cracks in the pavement whilst walking home is an 'obsession' we all recognise. Many children have rituals at bedtime but unless they are a significant source of distress to the individual or interfere severely with the child's social functioning they would not be seen as symptomatic of an obsessive/compulsive disorder.

As a disorder in childhood, obsessive/compulsive neurosis has been found to be relatively rare (Milby et al., 1983). Should a teacher be faced with a child experiencing this form of EBD, however, it can be very puzzling and alarming.

The main manifestation of this neurosis is either obsessions or compulsions or a combination of the two. Obsessions are repetitive impulses or thoughts that intrude and cannot be banished from conscious awareness. Compulsions involve repetitive stereotyped behaviours which the child, though recognising them as irrational, feels compelled to do.

Such children have been found to be generally of above average intelligence, and have a strict moral code which makes them feel irrationally guilty. Schwartz and Johnson (1985) quote the example of a girl, aged eight, who suddenly felt compelled to shake everything she encountered, e.g. tables, chairs and books, to see if they were solid. She confessed continually to minor wrong-doing and blew kisses to her toys to prevent them coming alive and doing her harm.

Both Judd (1965) and Adams (1973), and more recently Hollingsworth *et al.* (1980), identified seven characteristics that described children in this category:

(1) They are above average intelligence.
(2) The onset is sudden.
(3) Obsessive and compulsive symptoms occur together.
(4) Symptoms are disruptive to the environment.
(5) Children feel guilty.
(6) Children have an active fantasy life.
(7) There is no evidence of psychosis/mental illness.

All studies suggest the presence of aggression directed towards the parents and Adams found obsessional behaviour in 71.4 per cent of other members of the family.

As the condition is rare we may have no previous experience of a child suffering from obsessive, compulsive disorder so when we do encounter such a child it would be appropriate to refer him for specialised help. This may take the form of a programme of systematic desensitisation or a programme of responsive prevention undertaken in a clinical setting.

Somatoform disorders

Somatoform disorders present with symptoms that appear to be physical in nature but for which no organic basis can be found.

Childhood hysteria

The term hysterical neurosis has been used to refer to two somewhat different conditions:

- **Conversion reactions** – disorders in which there are physical symptoms suggestive of physical disorder, e.g. blindness, deafness, paralysis of various parts of the body for which no organic bases can be found.
- **Dissociative reactions** – characterised by an alteration in the individual's state of consciousness, e.g. amnesia, sleep-walking and multiple personality.

Dissociative reactions are found very rarely in children and conversion reactions are relatively rare. Goodyer (1981) has reported a figure of 0.5 per cent in a facility serving child inpatients.

Should we come across a child in school displaying the symptoms associated with hysteria we may rightly feel puzzled and concerned. The key factor when classifying a child as suffering from conversion disorder is the presence of a psychological trigger prior to the physical symptom. Maloney (1980) found that in a sample of 105 children with hysterical conversion reactions the onset in 97 per cent followed a significant family trauma. Of the same group 85 per cent were found to have a clinically depressed parent. Other common family variables were over-protectiveness on the part of the mother, marital problems, an ineffectual father and an over-investment by the parents in the child's somatic complaints.

It has been suggested that hysteria may be reflected in a specific pattern of personality characteristics including:

- self-centredness
- exhibitionism
- lack of emotional control
- seductiveness
- immaturity
- dependency.

Goodyer (1981) quotes the example of a nine-year old boy referred for partial loss of vision in both eyes, which came on suddenly and lasted from five minutes to two hours at any one time and could occur at any time of the day. No organic cause could be found but mother had a history of depression and father drank excessively. The loss of vision was observed to occur when father left the house following a marital argument.

In childhood, hysterical conversion reactions are found equally in boys and girls though in adults they are more often found in women.

Evidence as to how disturbing the disorder is to the child is conflicting. Kessler (1972), for example, found that children with conversion reactions were often quite comfortable with their symptoms and displayed what has been referred to as 'La belle indifférence'. On the other hand, Goodyer (1981) maintained that 'La belle indifférence' was the exception rather than the rule.

Depending on the extent to which the physical symptoms hamper the child's everyday life, he or she will continue to be educated in mainstream or referred for special education.

In both instances, treatment for the hysterical conversion reaction is likely to be undertaken in a clinical setting using behavioural methods, such as the use of positive reinforcement when the symptoms are controlled by the child or psychotherapy involving the whole family.

The teacher's role will be to be aware of the child's problems and the treatment which is being offered by other professionals and to co-operate with them wherever possible.

Affective disorders — childhood depression

The affective disorders of childhood are characterised by deep emotional disturbance. These disorders can involve extremes of mood, depression, elation or a combination of the two. Children may suffer mildly from these swings of mood in which case the teacher may be unaware of them or put them down to developmental stage or the natural temperament of the child. Indeed for many years it was assumed that only adults suffered from depression.

More recently studies have been reported which describe the presence of symptoms in children that would be classified as manic/depressive in adults, e.g. persistent crying, negative self-evaluations, talk of self-destruction. These symptoms have been found particularly in children who have been subjected to early separation from mother. Anyone who has seen the films made by the Robertsons about the two-year old going to hospital will recall the distressing cycle of protest, despair, depression and denial which the child exhibits.

Depression in childhood has been described (Cytryn and McKnew, 1972) as taking one of three forms:

- **Acute depressive reactions** Following a good pre-history of mental health the onset is preceded by some identifiable precipitating event. Often this involves a major loss, for example of a parent

through death or divorce or loss of affection or interest from some
important individual.

- **Chronic depressive reactions** The child has a poor pre-history and
  the symptoms appear gradually instead of suddenly. There is often
  a long history of separation and loss.
- **Masked depressive reactions** The depression is over-shadowed by
  other clinical features, e.g. hyperactivity, psychosomatic problems
  or delinquent behaviour. They are also usually related to loss in
  some part of the child's system.

Evidence from twin studies (Kashani *et al.*, 1981) supports the theory
that some children are genetically or bio-chemically disposed to
developing depressive disorders and the DSM 111 includes the
following symptoms in its criteria for depressive disorder, at least
four of which have been present nearly every day for at least two
weeks:

(1) Poor appetite or significant weight loss or increased appetite and
significant weight gain.
(2) Insomnia or hypersomnia.
(3) Extreme restlessness or extreme slowing down.
(4) Loss of interest or pleasure in usual activities.
(5) Loss of energy, easily tired.
(6) Feelings of worthlessness or excessive inappropriate guilt.
(7) Diminished ability to think or concentrate.
(8) Recurrent thoughts of death, suicide attempt.

It is likely that a pupil who is suffering from a depressive disorder will
either irritate a teacher, who may see no obvious reason for the
child's low spirits and low self-image, or call forth an over-protective
nurturing response in him, depending on his ability to identify with
the child's sense of loss.

Although a fairly high proportion of children referred for educational and psychiatric problems are diagnosed as depressive —
Pearce (1977) estimated between 15 per cent and 20 per cent —
within the population generally the incidence is much lower. Kashani
and Simonds (1979) arrived at a figure of 1.9 per cent.

The special needs of the depressed child are such, however, that
they can be met to some degree within school if the teacher is aware
of them. The teacher can be particularly effective in raising the child's
self-esteem through vigorous positive reinforcement of all his
strengths and potential strengths whilst, at the same time, helping

him to face the irrationality of his guilt and the internalisation of his anxieties.

Outside school, the child may be involved in individual, group or family therapy and it is helpful, if the teacher has knowledge of this, that he gives explicit and implicit support to the child's participation.

One extremely worrying aspect of childhood depression is its relationship to suicide. Studies of children who have attempted suicide have revealed a history of depression during the preceding months (Pfeffer, 1981). Pfeffer also found that the maximum risk for successful suicide is some two years after an initial unsuccessful attempt. Even though children sometimes appear to make a suicide attempt to gain attention or to manipulate their parents, suicide threats and attempts should always be taken seriously.

Rosenn (1982) identified ten popular **misconceptions** about suicidal behaviour in childhood as follows:

(1) Suicide under the age of six does not occur.
(2) Suicide in the child from six to puberty is extremely rare.
(3) True depression is not possible in childhood.
(4) Since children do not understand the irreversibility of death they cannot actually be considered suicidal.
(5) Suicide attempts are impulsive and unplanned.
(6) Children are not cognitively or physically able to implement a suicide plan effectively.
(7) Most suicide attempts in childhood are manipulative.
(8) Since most children make empty threats of suicide no one need be taken too seriously.
(9) Children do not usually have the means to kill themselves.
(10) There is always an overwhelming precipitating event before a child's attempt at suicide.

If a child feels depressed and talks of suicide to a teacher he should take it seriously and endeavour to seek professional help for the child both within and outside the school. The Samaritans have launched a scheme to help children as their figures are showing an increase in the number of young people who seek their help. The Charity's figures show that there were 139 suicides aged between 15 and 19 in 1989 – 114 male and 25 female, with three aged between 10 and 14. Every year one in a hundred girls aged between 15 and 19 takes an overdose in a suicide attempt.

The Samaritans now offer a teaching pack including material for topic work, drama, role-play and creative writing, all aimed at bringing troubled children back from the brink. Teachers in secondary education are particularly recommended to obtain their own resource pack from the Samaritans.

The neurotic disorders in childhood always run the risk of being over-looked in a school setting because they invariably cause more distress to the child himself than to others in his environment. The child internalises his problems and blames himself. If the teacher accepts this and then tries to work with the child in ways which will help him to gain a feeling that he has some control over what happens to him some of the extreme outcomes of a psychoneurotic disorder may be avoided.

2. PSYCHOSIS IN CHILDHOOD

Psychotic conditions are best described as those in which there is altered contact with reality and the child is attempting to adapt to a subjectively distorted concept of the world. This contrasts with the neurotic disorders in which the child is adapting, in an unhappy way, to his real life situation.

These are the most serious form of EBD from which a child can suffer and, in comparison with all other forms of EBD, are very rare. Wing *et al.* (1967) in the Middlesex survey found that the incidence was 4.5 per 10,000 children and Wilson (1986) also found that the incidence had remained at around 4.5 per 10,000 children.

It is the teacher in special education, therefore, who is most likely to come into contact with a child in this category. However, as these children are so severely disturbed and disturbing, when one does encounter them, a brief examination of the disorder is felt to be warranted in the present text.

For many years all psychotic disorders in children were referred to as childhood schizophrenia but more recently three types of disorder have been identified each with different distinguishing features and different ages of onset:

● **Early infantile autism** – the onset gradually from birth.
● **Symbiotic infantile psychosis** or **pervasive developmental disorder** – onset between 30 months and five years.
● **Childhood schizophrenia** – onset gradual between two to eleven years but usually in late childhood or early adolescence.

In infants and young children it is often difficult to be sure whether psychosis is present but the biggest clue is the presence of withdrawal from, or failure to make, normal, emotional contact with people.

Another difficulty is that onset of psychosis in childhood seriously distorts personality development and intellectual functioning and a child who fails to learn speech and motor function because of failure to make social contacts can appear to be mentally retarded.

Brain damage may in fact be responsible for some psychotic disorders (Barker, 1971) and theories of aetiology vary from the psychogenic to the bio-chemical.

From the teacher's point of view it is important to be aware of the identifying features of each condition and possible approaches to treatment.

Early infantile autism

'Autism' comes from the Greek word meaning 'self' and was first used in relation to childhood psychosis by Kanner in 1943 to describe a syndrome which is now referred to as 'early infantile autism'. It was first recognised in law in the Chronically Sick and Disabled Persons Act of 1970 and then singled out for attention by the DES in 1971 in its circular 'Education of Autistic Children', which required each LEA to indicate numbers of autistic children and provision made for them.

Kanner (1943) believed that the abnormal behaviours displayed by the child were a reflection of the 'cold' mother-child relationship and that the autistic child was potentially of normal intelligence. The syndrome was then defined (Rutter, 1978) as a cognitive-language impairment and later (Morgan, 1986) as a developmental disability arising from organic or neuropsychological factors. More recently (Welch, 1988) there has been a return to the Kanner hypothesis that autism is caused by faulty bonding between mother and child.

Whatever the proposed aetiology of the disorder there has been little disagreement over the presenting symptoms. Kanner (1943) suggested five criteria which were then amplified to nine by Creak (1961) and slightly altered by O'Gorman (1970).

Autism can only be diagnosed by taking a detailed history of the child's development and by closely observing the child's behaviour. Wilson (1986) gave the following comprehensive list of characteristics defining the disorder:

(1) The children are usually healthy and attractive but from an early age their social skills are deficient. They fail to smile, avoid eye contact, fail to give and receive non-verbal cues and seem to be in a world of their own.
(2) They insist on sameness and are upset by small changes in daily life.
(3) They become preoccupied with inanimate objects e.g. a spoon.
(4) They have severe language deficits — 50 per cent never develop intelligible speech — words are muddled or echoed repetitively.
(5) Many have an alert and intelligent facial expression.
(6) They suffer visual abnormalities including poor body image.
(7) They may have problems in sound perception though many love music.
(8) There are neurological abnormalities such as clumsiness, excessive standing on tip-toe, problems in discriminating left from right, yet some children can be agile and graceful.
(9) They may have 'islands' of skill, e.g. in memory, music, maths.

Insistence on the maintenance of 'sameness' in the environment, along with autistic 'aloneness' are the two principal diagnostic sign of early infantile autism. Unless the child introduces the changes, alterations in for example the position of the furniture or routines at bed-time can result in violent temper tantrums.

Since these children invest their emotional and intellectual energies in things rather than people they tend to ignore verbal suggestions and signs of praise or punishment.

The education of autistic children is highly specialised and usually takes place either in an SLD school, an EBD school or one of the few schools especially for autistic children sponsored by the National Society for Autistic Children (tel. 081-451 3844). As the prognosis for the autistic children who do not develop language is poor, communication needs to be given great emphasis and a high teacher/pupil ratio is essential.

Furneaux and Roberts (1977) concluded that above all teachers need to establish a good personal relationship with the autistic child in order to promote social and linguistic development. This could be reinforced in individual therapy sessions by the 'holding therapy' demonstrated by the Tinbergens (1983) in this country and Zappella (1979) in Italy.

Other forms of therapy include intense individual psychotherapy, drug-therapy and programmes of behavioural modification.

Symbiotic psychosis

This is a very rare syndrome chiefly characterised by symptoms of intense anxiety and panic over mother-child separation. Identified by Mahler (1968) it occurs between two-and-a-half years and five years of age and is usually preceded by a history of normal development in the first two years.

This child is, initially, the opposite to the autistic child who insists on 'aloneness'. The symbiotic child is unable to tolerate even short periods away from his mother and clings to her at all times. The panic reaction which characterises symbiotic psychosis may be triggered off by potential threats to the child's closeness to mother, e.g. the birth of another baby or going to nursery school. As symbiotic children are incapable of forming self-boundaries and seeing themselves as separate entities they fail to make relationships with anyone other than mother.

Minor changes in routine can throw this child into a panic in which he has severe temper tantrums often followed by bizarre ideas and behaviour. Mahler and Furman (1960) identified a symbiotic phase as a part of normal development, which is usually out-grown naturally. The symbiotic psychotic child, however, is stuck at this stage and, as the psychosis persists, other symptoms emerge. The child becomes withdrawn, disinterested in surroundings and his contact with reality weakens. As he develops the need for 'sameness' and his thinking becomes bizarre he starts to become indistinguishable from the child classified as autistic. Self-mutilating behaviour may start and abnormalities of speech and movement are quite common.

As with the autistic child, education is likely to be offered in a specialised setting and various forms of individual and behavioural therapy have been tried as well as the use of drugs – according to the theory of aetiology espoused by the therapist.

Childhood schizophrenia

Childhood schizophrenia usually occurs gradually between the ages of two and eleven but, most noticeably, at the onset of adolescence.

In most instances the onset is characterised by a profound decrease in interest in the external world of people and events and the child becomes absorbed with himself and loses contact with reality.

At times the child may be extremely withdrawn while at other

Figure 7.1 The three types of psychoses identifiable in childhood

Clinical Picture	Early infantile autism	Symbiotic infantile psychoses	Childhood schizophrenia
ONSET	Gradual from birth	Between two and one-half to five years after normal development.	Gradual between age two to eleven after period of normal development.
SOCIAL AND INTERPERSONAL	Failure to show anticipatory postural movements; extreme aloneness; insistence on sameness.	Unable to tolerate briefest separation from mother; clinging and incapable of delineating self.	Decreased interest in external world, withdrawal, loss of contact, impaired relations with others.
INTELLECTUAL AND COGNITIVE	High spatial ability; good memory; low IQ but good intellectual potential.	Bizarre ideation; loss of contact; thought disturbance.	Thought disturbance; perceptual problems; distorted time and space orientation; below average IQ.
LANGUAGE	Disturbances in speech; mutism, and if speech is present it is not used for communication. Very literal; delayed echolalia; pronoun reversal, I and Yes are absent till age six.		Disturbances in speech; mutism, and if speech is present, it is not used for communication.
AFFECT	Inaccessible and emotionally unresponsive to humans.	Severe anxiety and panic over separation from mother; low frustration tolerance; withdrawn and seclusive as psychosis persists.	Defect in emotional responsiveness and rapport, decreased, distorted, and/or inappropriate affect.
MOTOR	Head banging and body rocking; remarkable agility and dexterity; preoccupied with mechanical objects.		Bizarre body movements; repetitive and stereotyped motions; motor awkwardness; distortion in mobility.
PHYSICAL AND DEVELOPMENTAL PATTERNS	Peculiar eating habits and food preferences; normal EEG.	Disturbed normal rhythmic patterns.	Unevenness of somatic growth; disturbances of normal rhythmic patterns; abnormal EEG.
FAMILY	Aloof, obsessive and emotionally cold; high intelligence and educational and occupational levels; low divorce rate and incidence of mental illness.	Pathological mother who fosters the symbiosis.	High incidence of mental illness.

times he may show uncontrollable anger and destructive behaviour towards himself and others.

Intellectual and cognitive deficits have also been observed as part of the picture of schizophrenic children and Barker (1971) reports abnormalities of motor function with underactivity and overactivity but especially with bizarre movements and posturings, head-banging, whirling, rigid posturing.

Another prominent characteristic is language disorder due to the breakdown of associative links between thoughts. Bizarre thoughts or delusions and hallucinations or odd sensory experiences, e.g. hearing voices or 'seeing things', are sometimes present.

The incidence of childhood schizophrenia is low. Neal and Oltmans (1980) estimated about three to four children per 10,000. The classroom teacher is unlikely therefore to contact a child in this category during an average career. As the onset of the disorder, however, is often preceded by a prodromal or warning phase characterised by social isolation, odd behaviour such as talking to oneself or bizarre ideas, the observant teacher may be in a position to spot the incipient schizophrenic child and refer him, through official channels, for psychiatric assessment and help.

As the most recent theories of the aetiology of childhood schizophrenia favour the notion that genetic predisposition combined with environmental stress are responsible causal variables, therapy which combines the use of drugs and individual or family therapy is probably the best method of intervention.

A useful comparison of the three types of psychoses identifiable in childhood is presented in Figure 7.1.

Conclusion

In this chapter the rarest forms of EBD in children, the psychoneuroses and the psychoses, have been examined briefly.

Although the incidence of all these disorders is low, it has been considered important that teachers should be able to recognise them when they do occur and to have the confidence to take the necessary steps to seek specialised help for the child concerned.

Support and understanding for both the child and his family who are suffering the consequences of these distressing conditions will be vital and teachers should not underestimate or undervalue the role they can play in this area, if knowledgeable about and sensitive to the special psychological needs of the children involved.

CHAPTER EIGHT

Child Abuse

Introduction

All forms of emotional and behavioural disturbance are distressing to the child and to those in close contact with him such as teachers. There is one area of concern, however, that has only come into public recognition comparatively recently — the physical, emotional and sexual abuse of children, which arouses particularly strong feelings.

Although we have always been aware of the vulnerability of children owing to their total dependence both materially and emotionally on adults, there has been a reluctance to acknowledge that this vulnerability has been exploited in horrendous ways which are only in recent times coming to public attention.

The public enquiries into the deaths of Maria Colwell in 1973, Jasmine Beckford in 1984 and Kimberley in 1986, who were all fatally injured by their step-fathers, brought home the reality of physical abuse and neglect in the family. The Cleveland Report (1988) and the publicity surrounding Social Services' intervention in cases of suspected child sexual abuse in places like Nottingham, Rochdale and the Orkneys, has similarly underlined the existence of sexual and emotional abuse within the family. Subjects which have been taboo are now aired publicly and, as teachers, we can no longer seek to ignore them or to stand aside.

Arguments as to whether teachers should be involved in what happens to their pupils beyond the confines of the classroom and school were addressed firmly by the Government when they specified that the professional duties of the teacher should include:

> maintaining good order and discipline among pupils and safe-guarding their health and safety;
> providing guidance and advice to pupils on education and social matters . . . including information about sources of more expert

advice on specific questions;
communicating and consulting with the parents of pupils.

This overall pastoral obligation of the teacher was reinforced in relation to child abuse by the DES circular No. 4/88, July 1988, entitled *Working Together For The Protection Of Children From Abuse: Procedures Within The Education Service*. The circular with the accompanying DHSS booklet *Working Together*, a guide to arrangements for inter-agency co-operation for the protection of children from abuse, stressed the importance of the role it is possible for teachers to play.

In this chapter, therefore, physical abuse and neglect, sexual and emotional abuse, will be examined in the school context. Particular reference will be made to the legal position, identification and disclosure of abuse, effects on the child and the teacher's role in prevention and constructive support for the child.

The legal position

Primary responsibility for the protection of children from abuse rests with social services departments, the NSPCC and the police. Other agencies in a position to help include the education service, family practitioners, the probation service, youth and health services.

Each LEA should designate a senior member of staff to co-ordinate action within the school and to liaise with other agencies. In all cases where teachers, or other members of staff, suspect abuse of any form, they should report their suspicions to the designated member of staff, who will then follow the procedures laid down by the LEA. This usually entails contacting a named member of the local Social Services Department and a named officer of the Education Department. Staff should note carefully what they have observed, describing physical injuries in detail and quoting comments by the child concerned.

The DES emphasise that the designation of a co-ordinating teacher should not be seen as diminishing the role of all teachers in being alert to signs of abuse.

It is not the responsibility of school staff to make enquiries of parents or guardians. It is for the statutory agencies – SSDs, the NSPCC and the police – to investigate suspected abuse. However, in schools where there is a good relationship between staff and parents, information may be volunteered by parents and this should be recorded and passed on to the appropriate agency.

The law regarding measures which can be taken is complex and a thorough understanding of it is not usually within the teacher's domain. However, it is important to know that in a *desperately dangerous situation* a teacher can apply for a Place of Safety order, so that a child at risk does not go home from school; and also that teachers do have the right to seek legal advice from their LEA Legal Services Department.

In each area covered by a social services department a central register must be maintained, which lists all the children in the area who have been abused or who are considered to be at risk of abuse and who, therefore, are currently the subject of an inter-agency plan to protect them. The term 'child abuse' in this context is used to cover neglect, physical abuse, sexual abuse and emotional abuse.

The register should be managed by a senior social worker and will provide a central point of speedy inquiry for professional staff such as teachers, who are worried about a child and want to know whether the child is the subject of an inter-agency protection plan.

Physical abuse and neglect

Although the maltreatment of children has been recorded throughout history, it was only with Kempe *et al.*'s (1962) classical description of the 'battered child syndrome' that any real interest was shown in the subject.

- Physical child abuse generally refers to non-accidental injury (NAI).
- Child neglect implies the failure to act properly in safe-guarding the health, safety and well-being of the child. It can encompass physical neglect, nutritional neglect and emotional neglect.
- Maltreatment is usually used to refer to both abuse and neglect.

At its simplest level, physical abuse consists of a parent or caretaker deliberately injuring the child. An NSPCC definition (Baher *et al.*, 1976) of child physical abuse is:

> . . . where the nature of the injury is not consistent with the account of how it has occurred, or other factors indicate that it was probably caused non-accidentally.

Estimates of the level of child physical abuse are being constantly revised. A December 1985 NSPCC press release estimated 7,000 cases of child physical abuse per year. For the year 1989 a similar release estimated 10,500 cases involving children aged from 0 – 16 years. It would not be unusual, therefore, for a teacher to have in class at some point a child who is suffering, or who is at risk of suffering, from physical abuse and neglect at home.

There are no particular 'types' of abusing parent, as Frude (1980) expressed it:

> There is no universal personality characteristic of the abusing parent, nor is there a universal sociological factor.

Frude did, however, identify certain common characteristics of abusing families and these are as follows:

(1) One or both parents have been subjected to violence themselves as children.
(2) One or both parents have had an unhappy, disrupted and insecure childhood.
(3) One or both parents are addicted to drugs, alcohol or are psychotic.
(4) There is a record of violence between parents.
(5) Another child has already been abused, or suffered an unexplained death.
(6) The pregnancy was unwanted; the baby was rejected at birth or soon after.
(7) Failure of early bonding.
(8) Both parents are under 20 years of age, immature for their years and socially isolated.
(9) The family live in poor housing and on low income.
(10) The family is suffering from multiple deprivation.

Those of us who have brought up babies and young children will recall with horror moments when, worn out from sleepless nights or feeling ill or worried ourselves, we have viewed our off-spring with some degree of irritation if not anger. It then becomes partly comprehensible — though totally reprehensible — when, for instance, a single parent suffering from multiple deprivation becomes violent towards a child.

This emphasises the need for all those in daily contact with children to pick up any warning signals which are being sent out by the child and/or family and to seek ways of providing support which may avert catastrophe.

A new charity called Newpin has been established, with some assistance from the Department of Health, where mothers who are reaching the end of their tether with a child can drop in and seek

120

support from other mothers who have experienced and conquered similar difficulties. Each woman is offered the opportunity of a weekly session of group psychotherapy plus sessions in child care and life skills. The telephone number to contact is 071-703 5271.

Recognising the maltreated child

Depending on the particular duties a teacher undertakes in school, e.g. supervising changing for PE or games, he will be in a position to spot the physical manifestations of physical abuse listed in Figure 8.1.

If one is not in a position to notice the physical signs, which are often deliberately placed out of sight by the abuser, there are certain general indicators which the observant teacher might pick up. Such warning signals may include:

- mental retardation or neurological impairment not explicable through trauma or head injury
- growth failure — 'failure to thrive syndrome'
- frozen, watchful behaviour
- clinging behaviour
- impaired speech and language
- attention-seeking behaviour
- aggressive behaviour
- parents with unlikely explanations for injuries
- learning disorders.

Not surprisingly the physically-abused child often has very low self-esteem and feels worthless. His often aggressive and attention-seeking behaviour makes it hard for him to make friends and his misery at home is compounded by misery at school.

Green (1968) postulated that early physical abuse may enhance the development of pain dependent behaviour. The child may become accident prone, indulge in self-destructive behaviour or establish a pattern of inviting harm and playing the victim (Bender, 1976). Other writers stress the tendency of the abused child to identify with the abuser and to develop violent behaviour as a character trait (Galdston, 1975).

In a detailed study of abused children Martin and Beezley (1976) noted nine characteristics and behaviours in their sample as follows:

(1) impaired capacity to enjoy life

Figure 8.1 Recognising physical abuse

IS THERE EVIDENCE OF PHYSICAL INJURY?
(If any of the following symptoms are identified or suspected, ensure that the child receives a medical examination, as soon as possible)

1. **Bruises to face and head** — cheek, black eyes, damaged upper lip (inside especially), ear, side of skull
2. **'Finger-tip', hand bruises** — especially on trunk, limbs (grasping), fingers or hand wheals on any part
3. **Bite marks** — anywhere, usually soft tissues
4. **Inner thighs** — bruises, scratches, wheals, instruments, 'whip' marks
5. **Bruising lower back** — buttocks, backs of thighs, calves
6. **Small cutaneous haemorrhages** (petechiae) — anywhere
7. **Weapon marks**
8. **Ligature marks** — strangling, tying up
9. **Bizarre marks**
10. **Multiple soft tissue injuries.**
    (*Remember*: When children fall they bruise bony prominent parts and *not* soft, fleshy parts. Children under 2 years of age should not show bruises. Contrary to popular belief, children do not pepper themselves with bruises when learning to walk.)
11. **Burns** — for example:
    (a) Cigarette burns, fresh or scarred
    (b) Linear, e.g. pokers, bars of electric fire
    (c) Curious shaped objects
    (d) Dry contact burns (held near source of heat)
    (e) Held *in* or *on* fire
    (f) Scalds — (i) Hot liquid thrown or poured; (ii) Immersion ('ducking') in bath or bowl
       A typical *accidental* scald 'cascades' on to *front* of child catching prominent parts (head, face, arms, upper chest, thighs), and spares the recessed areas (neck, lower abdomen, groins, elbow creases).
12. **Bony injuries** —
    (a) May be completely hidden
    (b) May be associated with swelling and tenderness of overlying parts
    (c) Child may limp, refuse to walk, avoid using or moving affected part
    (d) Often multiple
13. **Brain and eye injuries** — Often requires special examination or investigation for their detection. Fits of drowsiness are important signs.
14. **Internal injuries** — Rare, may involve chest or abdomen. Likely to be associated with cutaneous injury in same area.
15. **Poisoning** — Difficult to diagnose. Drowsiness or peculiar behaviour might suggest this.

(2) psychiatric symptoms e.g. enuresis, tantrums, hyperactivity, bizarre behaviour
(3) low self-esteem
(4) school learning problems
(5) withdrawal
(6) opposition
(7) hypervigilance
(8) compulsivity
(9) pseudo-mature behaviour.

If a classroom teacher observes a child to be displaying any or a combination of any of the above symptoms of abuse, he may be able to give the child an opportunity to confide in him. The abuse may still be at the neglect stage and, if reported, may be curbed before serious physical abuse takes place. The NSPCC gives the following clues to neglect and urges concerned adults to pass on their observations and worries:

- Children who are left on their own indoors – in law a person under sixteen cannot be held responsible for the care of children
- Children who are wandering the streets
- Children who are regularly left in charge of their younger brothers and sisters
- Children who are unusually withdrawn and miserable
- Children who are unusually aggressive
- Children who are desperate for affection
- Children who are dirty, smelly and underfed
- Children who have lingering illnesses, which are not attended to
- Children who have serious difficulties at school.

The problem of child neglect is serious. The NSPCC estimates that each year 150–200 children die following abuse and neglect and the number of cases of neglect reported to them exceeds 6,000 per annum. The teacher should not feel diffident therefore about reporting to a senior colleague any possible evidence that a child is being seriously neglected or physically abused at home. The significance of the abuse is that something is going radically wrong in the family and the concerned teacher, whilst acting primarily in the interests of the child, may, by contacting the right agency such as social services, be helping to gain vital aid and support for the whole family.

Charles (1983), from her experience as a social worker with physically abused children, identified certain popularly held misconceptions about child physical abuse. Abusing parents need not be conspicuously different from ordinary parents and may not appear as monsters with two heads or even be suffering from obvious life stress. The need to abuse a child may meet a a psychological need in the parent. The presence of an unharmed child or children in the family does not indicate that all children may be safe there. Finally, we are not right to assume that unless we know how injuries occurred they must have been accidental. Abusing parents can be good at thinking up plausible explanations for NAI and we should not think that any story, however unlikely, equals an explanation.

Prevention and constructive support

It takes an exercise of the imagination to enter the world of the abused child and even more so to enter the world of the abuser but if we consider that many abused children grow up to be abusers we, in education, may be in a strong position to help to prevent this. The DES circular (July, 1988) suggests that, in the longer term, schools may be able to play a part in the prevention of child abuse through the teaching they offer. Courses in personal and social education can help young people to develop more realistic attitudes towards the responsibilities of adult life, including parenthood.

The inclusion of a child care course in the curriculum can involve the children in discussion and practical exercises to do with the physical and emotional care of their future children. It also enables the child who is suffering from inadequate parenting or abuse to discuss, albeit in the third person, the anxieties and pain from which he suffers. The imaginative teacher will be able to construct role-play situations for the children to enact in which each child can play in turn both the aggressor and the victim. This can help the physically abused child, who may have developed pain dependency or aggressive behaviour modelled on parents, to cathart his strong feelings in a 'safe' situation.

The teacher who knows that he has a pupil in his class who is on the Child Protection Register will be keen to take an active part in the inter-agency protection plan and should, wherever possible, be allowed to attend multi-disciplinary case-conferences on this particular child.

Because the physical safety of the child, due to the high mortality rate and incidence of brain injury associated with the battered child syndrome, has, understandingly, taken priority, the emotional and educational effects on the child have sometimes been overlooked. The child for his own protection may have been removed, sometimes suddenly, from his home and is likely to present at school as highly emotionally and behaviourally disturbed, tending to be extremely withdrawn and compliant or extremely aggressive and hyperactive.

The caring teacher, anxious to create a healing atmosphere in the classroom for this child, needs to assess, with some finesse, his particular needs. A child who has been reared in cold isolation may be easily overwhelmed by 'effusive caring' from his teacher. On the other hand, the child may demonstrate an over-eager and sometimes embarrassing need for physical closeness and affection. Although he dislikes the harsh treatment he receives from one or both parents, he may still wish to have respect shown to them as they are very much a symbol of him and his worth as a human being.

Whilst an abused child would naturally fear over-discipline, he may feel very insecure without any boundaries and would look to the teacher to provide a well-defined and consistent set of rules within which he can feel safe. The teacher is thrown back again, therefore, onto attempting to understand each individual child's special emotional and behavioural needs and tailoring his teaching and classroom management of the child to those needs wherever possible.

The teacher should have resources within and outside the school to whom he can turn for guidance and for emotional support in dealing with the sad plight of the neglected and physically abused child. The continued development of well-functioning area child protection teams, reinforced by the Children Act 1989, should allow participation by relevant teachers and accord them the respect and status they deserve as caring professionals.

Child sex abuse

The existence of child sex abuse is even more shocking and hard to accept than the existence of child physical abuse, so it is not surprising that, when first confronted with it, our reactions are similar to those we experience in the shock of, for instance, a bereavement. The reactions to this type of shock follow a predictable pattern (Murray-Parkes and Weiss, 1983). The first response is denial. For example the teacher may say to himself, 'If it is really so widespread why is it only recently that it's in the news? I don't believe it! Well if it does happen, it's not in this school which is in a 'nice' middle-class area. I know my pupils and I would have known if it existed. It just doesn't happen!'

When increasing evidence forces one to give up the defence-mechanism of denial, anger is the next likely response. Not only is anger expressed against the abuser, often the father or step-father, but also against the mother — 'who must have known it was happening and did nothing about it'.

When this reaction starts to fade it is replaced with depression and a feeling of helplessness and inadequacy. If this depression gives way to despair and apathy it is destructive, but if it is channelled into empathy for the child it can lead to the next stage, which is acceptance.

Constructive acceptance does not imply passive resignation but is translated into 'what can I do about it?' Many adults, not just teachers, never come out of the denial stage in relation to child sex abuse, so it is not surprising that research has shown (Ward, 1984) that, from his findings at that time, children, on average, reported sexual abuse at least nine times before any action was taken. Until recently sexual abuse has been a taboo subject and it is still, as Porter (1984) maintains, surrounded by secrecy:

> Sexual abuse occurs in secret, is kept secret by the family, and is kept secret by society's attitudes and taboos.

Definitions of child sex abuse vary. The most widely quoted definition is that of Kempe and Kempe (1978):

> The involvement of developmentally immature children and adolescents in sexual activities they do not truly comprehend, to which they are unable to give informed consent, or that violates the social taboos of family roles.

The Incest Survivors' Campaign, seeking to underline the belief that sexual abuse is essentially about the misuse of power, offers the alternative definition:

> Sexual molestation of a child by any person that the child sees as a figure of trust and authority.

Incidence

For many years, figures concerning the incidence of sexual abuse of children were masked by what is now believed to vast under-reporting. In 1984 a Mori poll found that, in a sample of 2,000 adults over the age of fifteen, 10 per cent claimed to have had a sexually abusing experience in childhood with an adult (Baker and Duncan, 1985).

In 1985, Nash and West in a study of adult women used two sample groups. The first sample was taken from a general practitioner's patient list and the second from a group of students. They found that 42 per cent of the GP group and 54 per cent of the student group reported some degree of child sexual contact.

The national estimate published by the NSPCC for the year 1989 was 6,600 cases of child sexual abuse in the age range 0 – 16 years.

Finkelhor's research (1980) in the USA indicated that 19 per cent of women and nine per cent of men report an experience of sexual abuse that appears to have had long-term harmful psychological effects.

What we know of the sexual abuse of boys is limited. The Baker and Duncan study (1985) indicated that eight per cent of men report instances from their childhood years, with the peak age being in their early teens. These men were found to be more at risk of on-going abuse but less likely to be the victims of more than one abuser than girls. It is generally considered that boys are even less likely to report abuse than girls and that the official figures do not reflect the true picture. Monaco and Gaier (1988) reported that male victims felt that since they are 'men' they should have been in control of the situation, and because of a feeling of shame they are reluctant to disclose that they have been sexually abused.

It is probably true to say that the public generally is not really aware that boys can easily become victims. Childline posters tend to feature girls and, until recently, there has been no rape crisis counselling on offer for men. Society's definition of masculinity still does not expect males to express feelings of 'dependency, fear, vulnerability or helplessness' (Nasjleti, 1980). Boys may also see their abuse as signs that they are homosexual. This can lead to under-reporting, particularly when boys are aware of society's intolerance towards homosexuals and of references to AIDS as the 'gay plague'.

There are many reasons to account for the difficulty that children have in being able to disclose what has happened to them. Firstly, children often do not have the vocabulary and/or permission to talk about the sort of thing that is happening to them. More importantly, when children do pluck up the courage to confide in a trusted adult, the adult has difficulty in believing their story.

Most abused children are subjected to threats of what will happen to them if they 'tell' and, of course, many are offered bribes not to divulge what is happening. Children may even believe the abusive experience to be 'normal' within an affectionate family relationship or it may be the only way in which they are shown love and physical affection.

The consequences of 'telling', e.g. father going to prison or the child being taken away from home, may have been painted all too graphically to them, and some media cover may have reinforced this, so it is not surprising that a belief exists that many cases still go undiscovered and unreported.

The teacher's role

For teachers who are relatively new to the whole distressing subject of child sexual abuse, the following points are offered as some introductory information and advice:

(1) Sexual abuse does not have to be violent to be abuse.

(2) Most children are abused by someone they know.

(3) Children often have difficulty in 'telling' a parent, so may choose their teacher as the most trusted adult they know.

(4) Children rarely lie about such a serious matter.

(5) It is your duty as a teacher to pass on disclosures to the school's designated representative.

(6) Your own feelings about the subject will be highly charged and you will need to discuss these with someone you trust.

(7) If a child has found the courage to confide in you, she will continue to look to you for support through the subsequent proceedings, even though you have referred the matter on.

The Government in Circular 4/88 emphasised the need for training to enable the awareness and recognition of child abuse:

> Acknowledging the many pressures on curriculum time in initial training, the Secretary of State nevertheless expects that this preparation will include awareness and recognition of child abuse, and the appropriate procedures as outlined in this Circular (para 23).

For those of us who trained prior to this recent Order (1987), and especially for those teachers designated as having responsibility for liaison and co-ordination within the school, programmes of in-service training will be essential. Inter-disciplinary conferences and professional contact with those more experienced will also be of value.

Warning signs of sexual abuse

There are many lists of warning signs indicative of sexual abuse, some of which are physical and more likely to come to light in a medical setting than in school. Damage to the genital areas and anal areas, itching, soreness, discharge or unexplained bleeding for instance, may well not come to the attention of the teacher.

There are some indications, however, which would be well within the teacher's powers of observation and should always serve as a warning light and which may need further investigation. In very young children the following behaviours might be indicative of abuse:

- Excessive masturbation and heightened genital awareness
- Sexual acting out behaviour to adults the child likes, as he

innocently associates sexual behaviour with nurturance and affection

- Simulated sexual activity between the victim and younger children
- Simulated sexual activity with dolls and stuffed animals
- Fear of being alone with adults of either sex
- Hurting younger children, pets or being destructive to objects
- Self-mutilation – head-banging, picking at sores, hitting at genitals
- Displaying sexual knowledge beyond their age, e.g. being able to describe erection, ejaculation, male masturbation and oral sex
- Expression through drawings or play, of advanced sexual knowledge

Amongst the many warning signals in older children the following behaviours should give rise to concern:

- Inappropriate sexual behaviour for the child's age, promiscuous behaviour and pre-occupation with sex
- Hinting at sexual activity through words, play or drawings: or at the presence of severe family conflict and family secrets, but seeming fearful of outside intervention.
- Sudden changes in mood – becoming either depressed or withdrawn, or disobedient, attention-seeking, restless
- Changes in eating habits – over-eating or under-eating (Anorexia has recently come to be associated in some instances with sexual abuses.)
- Hysterical attacks
- Truancy or running away from home
- Suicide attempts or self-mutilation
- Dependence on alcohol or drugs
- Inability to concentrate, learning difficulties, or a sudden drop in school performance
- Marked reluctance to participate in physical activity or to change clothes for PE or games
- Regular avoidance or fear of school medicals
- First to arrive at school
- Last to depart from school
- Frequent lateness or absence
- Inappropriate reactions to in-school preventive work

Among this plethora of warning signals, many of which might equally be indicative of other forms of EBD, how is the perplexed teacher to choose the most significant?

Milner and Blyth (1989), in their excellent book *Coping with Child Sexual Abuse: A Guide for teachers*, suggest that the most significant signs from the teacher's point of view are:

(1) Picking up veiled references which a child makes through writing, art, play and drama – older pupils being able to discuss in small groups 'hypothetical' situations which in fact apply to them.
(2) Inappropriate sexual behaviour for the child's age.
(3) Not wanting to go home even when quite ill.
(4) Pseudo-mature behaviour, particularly in girls who take on the wife/mother role at home.

Children vulnerable to abuse and the perpetrators of abuse

The commonest type of problem concerns 13 and 14-year old girls who are being abused by their fathers, step-fathers, brothers, step-brothers or even grandfathers.

Mother/son and mother/daughter incest are both rarely reported and, as previously indicated, the abuse of boys is considered to be vastly under-reported. Incest Crisis Line figures state that:

> 30% of children in care are abused children; 99% of rent boys, i.e. boy prostitutes, are abused children and 75% of prostitutes, some still of school age, have been abused children.

Children with special educational needs form a particularly vulnerable group of children where child sex abuse is concerned. Physically dependent children are used to being handled by adults and Thornton (1981), for example, describes how, as a child with cerebral palsy, no-one ever asked her if she minded having her body touched. Children with severe learning difficulties are vulnerable because their carers tend to relate to them as very young children even when they are maturing physically. Children who have been emotionally deprived or physically maltreated are often desperate for warmth and affection and will sometimes happily collude with sexual abuse to obtain these favours.

Morgan (1987) suggests that special handling techniques should be explained to all SEN staff and that sex education should not be viewed as irrelevant for children with special educational needs. She further suggests that children prone to hugging and kissing indiscriminately should be taught how to shake hands, as a means of protection to the teacher as well as to the child.

Certain characteristics within families make children more vulnerable to sexual abuse, and some of these are related to the personal and socio-economic background of the parent/parents. Mrazek and Kempe (1981) suggest, for example:

- Was the child unwanted?
- Has the child been in care at any stage?
- Was there early separation of the child and mother?
- Are the caretakers very young?
- Is there any stress caused by low income?
- Is there any evidence of marital/relationship difficulties?
- Are there any other persons residing at or visiting the household who could constitute a threat to a child?

The inference, however, that sexual abusers are likely to come from low socio-economic backgrounds has not been supported by research evidence. The Kempes (1978) found that the abused children they interviewed represented the children of professionals and white and blue collar workers, as well as the poor, in a way that reflected a true cross-section of the community.

Forward and Buck (1981) concluded that the abusing families came from 'every economic, cultural, racial, educational, religious and geographical background. They are doctors, policemen, prostitutes, secretaries, artists and merchants. They are happily married and four times divorced . . . they are emotionally stable and they have multiple personalities.'

Ward (1984) found in his research that up to 50 per cent of offenders are the actual father; 25 per cent or more from the affinity system in which the child lives. However much we emphasise to children, and rightly so, that they should not trust or go off with strangers, in reality, they are far more vulnerable to abuse from the people they know.

The other group of perpetrators of child sex abuse are the paedophiles, who choose their families, their jobs and their friends with a view to gaining access to children. Their number is unknown but Righton (1981) found that they are almost always men and, in the main, indicate a preference for boys. Far from being odd, isolated individuals, they are often intelligent, professional men with some standing.

There is no stereotype, therefore, of the child sexual abuser or the abused child. This makes it even more difficult for us as teachers to see the problem clearly. The possibility also exists, of course, that some of our colleagues could have suffered abuse as a child or may even be an abuser. It is little wonder then that we experience the whole field of child sexual abuse as a minefield and are right to do so.

Ritual child abuse

In Rochdale (1989) it was a classroom teacher's report on the disturbed behaviour and bizarre stories recounted by one of her six-year old boy pupils – including tales of murdered 'ghost babies' – which sparked investigations by social workers into the possible existence of ritual child abuse. The publicity surrounding the subsequent action taken by the social services who, as the media portrayed it, used a 'dawn raid' to remove children from home, together with Mr Justice Brown's criticism of the social workers involved, will no doubt serve to deter teachers in future from reporting suspicions of this nature.

If the existence of child sex abuse can give rise to denial in the average member of the public, the existence of highly organised ritualistic, satanic abuse is even more difficult to contemplate. Professionals in a number of services have been accused of whipping up hysteria and the stories children have told have been put down to fantasy or the result of watching 'video nasties'. It is not a crime to be a witch or a satanist but the practices in which satanic rings are alleged to have indulged certainly breach a number of different laws: indecent assault, rape, buggery, sexual relations with a junior, procuring miscarriage.

Hard evidence of ritual child abuse has been hard to come by in a climate where it is felt that children have been brain-washed by over zealous social workers into making false accusations.

In Nottingham, however, in 1989 the police had evidence of gross sexual abuse and cruelty in an extended family involving nine adults and 23 children. Ritual abuse scarcely featured in the trial – it was filtered out by the prosecution. The information came out when the children individually, and quite separately, told their foster parents about it. In wardship hearings held on these cases five High Court judges decided that ritual abuse *had* occurred. Charges of brain-washing were 'ludicrous' said one judge.

In an article in the Guardian (3/11/1990), Valerie Sinason quotes a consultant psychiatrist, Dr Judith Trowell, as saying:

As we began our work, there was an enormous struggle to convince people that child sexual abuse existed. Now with the advent of satanic abuse 'ordinary' child sexual abuse becomes diminished and devalued in contrast.

As we reel from the uncovering of paedophile rings and the knowledge that abusers come from all classes and professions, there is perhaps an unconscious interest in keeping up an hysterical attack on satanic abuse to minimise the impact of 'ordinary' child sexual abuse.

Whatever stand we take personally, as teachers it is still our legal duty and obligation to pass on to the relevant member of staff any revelations made to us by the children, however far-fetched and disturbing they may seem. Teachers unsure of what to make of children's stories or play can discuss their problem with Kidscape (tel: 071-488 0488), the charity which promotes child safety. There is another organisation run by SCOGAC which has a help line for teachers two days a week, enabling them to discuss their concerns in confidence (tel: 091-969 4808, Thursdays and Fridays, from 10.00am – 4pm). These contacts should not be used as a substitute for following DES and LEA procedures but can provide a much needed source of personal support and advice.

Understandably, in the light of the sensational press coverage of cases like those in Rochdale and the Orkney islands, teachers are reluctant to take steps which might involve even more traumatic experiences for the child concerned. Teachers may well suppose that if they pass on the information the situation may not be handled sensitively. Michelle Elliott of Kidscape compares this dilemma with a lorry rolling towards a child who is in the middle of the road. You want to save the child's life. You throw the child out of the way but in so doing the child breaks his leg. Which is more important? That the child's life is saved at the expense of a broken leg or that the child should take a life and death risk from the advancing lorry?

In the case of sexual abuse, difficult as the decision is to make, like the lorry analogy there is no real contest when one considers the long-term psychological damage that persistent abuse can cause. Over and above the emotional pain, a female victim may also have valid fears about pregnancy, venereal disease and AIDS. There is really no ambiguity then over whether teachers should report disturbing signs of child sexual abuse.

The effects of child sexual abuse

There is no general agreement about the impact in adult life of child sexual abuse. Kempe and Kempe (1978) found that not all individuals had been harmed by a long standing incestuous relationship. Conversely, Freud (1981) maintained:

> Where the chances of harming a child's normal development are concerned, it (i.e. sexual abuse) ranks higher than abandonment, neglect, physical maltreatment or any other form of abuse. It would be a mistake to underrate the implication or frequency of its actual occurrence.

The matter is complicated by the fact that children may acquiesce, co-operate and sometimes even enjoy the sexual experience (Yates, 1982); but sexual abuse that takes place in a context of warmth, bribery, special attention, privileges and extreme secrecy, may be as psychologically traumatic and bewildering to a child as violent sexual abuse (Fritz et al., 1981).

Girls may seek to sexualise all their relationships and become promiscuous. They may also have difficulty in expressing anger either at their father or at their mother for failing to protect them. This can turn into self-destructive behaviour. Suicidal attempts are not uncommon especially in families that have disintegrated and where the mother has clearly blamed the abused child (Goodwin, 1981).

Studies of the effects on adults of child sexual abuse identify three major groups:

(1) Promiscuous adults often with alcohol or drug abuse problems
(2) Sexually cold adults who are unable to form lasting sexual and emotional relationships
(3) Adults who report no lasting effects.

Tsai et al., (1979) found that the groups with clinical problems, groups 1 and 2, had usually been abused over a long period and actual intercourse had been involved. The group with no symptoms in later life had had support from friends and family during childhood and had not been blamed for the events. They had also found sexual partners in adulthood who were sympathetic and understanding.

If, as teachers then, we are aware that one of our pupils is the subject of sexual abuse our contribution to making her feel she is not to blame and that we still value her can help to minimise the feelings of contamination, guilt and dirtiness, which adult victims reveal they felt as children.

As sexually abused children often become parents who abuse physically and sexually their own children, our efforts to understand and offer a therapeutic classroom and personal management of these particular EBD children can also be seen as a contribution to preventive work for the next generation.

Handling disclosures

When a child has indicated, directly or through veiled hints and 'interesting' stories or drawings, that she has some confidences she wishes to share with you, great care and thought should be given to how you are going to handle this situation. Remember that you may be the first person the child has decided to tell. In his study of incest, Chesterman (1985) found that teachers were told first more than any other group of adults.

If the school has a clearly defined policy on child abuse and there is open discussion amongst the staff it should be possible to designate an area within the school where a teacher can take a child in the confidence that they will not be disturbed. Ideally the area would be private, carpeted and warm, equipped with comfortable soft furniture, puppets, toys and materials for drawing, writing and painting.

The teacher has to recognise that the experience is going to be painful for both himself and the child. The initial task is to give the child the confidence that she will be believed. It is *not* helpful to pretend that what the child is telling you is not disturbing or even shocking, but rather to openly recognise with the child that it has taken great courage to talk about it. The teacher should then seek to relieve the child of any guilt or the feeling that the abuse had in any way been invited by her. Reassurance needs to be given that this does happen to other children and that there are ways in which help can be sought.

If the child tries to swear you to secrecy explain, from the outset, that this is so serious that you will have to tell at least one other person who will be needed to assist in obtaining the help she requires. The teacher cannot make promises that he is not in a position to keep so he must be honest about the possible consequences, as far as he can make a judgment about them.

In discussing the sexual parts of the body and any sexual acts implied it may be necessary to use the child's own terminology. All questions in any case should be phrased in simple direct language that the child can readily understand. When helping a very young child or a child with poor verbal skills, the teacher needs to be prepared to use dolls, especially anatomically correct dolls, a doll's house and furniture, drawings and paintings etc.

Above all, remember that the child in all probability still loves the abusing parent — though not the abusive act itself — so respect this point of view and accept the child's natural ambivalence in this matter.

It is also necessary, on each and every occasion, to keep a record. If the teacher is the first person to hear from a child about sexual abuse it becomes particularly important to make an accurate recording of precisely what was said and acted out in the disclosure. This may have the added advantage for the child in not having to keep repeating the story, which can obviously be traumatic in itself.

Finally, the teacher is advised, as mentioned previously, to use the procedure laid down by the DES and the LEA to refer the matter to the right sources and be prepared to give long-term support to any pupil, if there is a recognised need for this, long after the initial disclosure.

It may well be that after disclosure the child is not easy to manage and Browne and Finkelhor (1986) have suggested that a child's reactions are likely to fall into one of the following four patterns of response:

(1) The child is sexually traumatised and either shows terror of sex or is actively promiscuous.
(2) The child feels overwhelmingly betrayed and loses all capacity to trust.
(3) The child feels powerless and helpless in an aggressive world.
(4) The child feels stigmatised – a girl may be called a 'slut' by peers, who know of her experience: a boy may be called a 'filthy little sod'.

Should a child who has made a disclosure to a teacher subsequently withdraw the allegations, it requires an extra effort of imagination and patience to understand this. As Bentovim (1987) has made clear, abusing families have a vested interest in trying to reinstate the family secret and sometimes all family members, including mother, rally around the perpetrator to protect the reputation of the whole family. Children who are ostracised by their family are under great pressure to withdraw their accusations. The teacher may be left feeling totally foolish in a situation like this and will need to understand how the child concerned has not meant to make a fool of him but has simply chosen the lesser evil of not being blamed for breaking up the family.

Teachers faced with the emotional and behavioural difficulties presented by children who have been abused need to acknowledge the anger, disgust and fear which this experience can provoke in them and, with the help of colleagues and members of an Area Protection Team, be helped to play a constructive role in the child's rehabilitation, without too much personal heartache.

Preventive work

As the DES Circular 4/88 suggests, it is possible to use the school curriculum as a means of building up an awareness of the possible dangers of abuse and ways of avoiding it. Safety teaching is a standard part of primary education and this can, with imagination, be designed in such a way as to include aspects of the world where children face risk. These include fire, electricity, road traffic, approaches by strangers, bullies and being touched in a disturbing way by people they know.

The whole question of appropriate and inappropriate touching is very well illustrated in the Kidscape literature, which suggests ways in which responsible adults, such as parents and teachers, can discuss this with children without it being overwhelming or frightening in its own right. *The Kidscape Primary Kit* (Michelle Elliott and Kidscape) contains five step-by-step teaching manuals, a video for parents and teachers, templates and 300 posters and leaflets, which can be freely photocopied. It is available from Kidscape, 82 Brook Street, London WIY IYG.

There are also several videos available to teachers, e.g. *Kids can Say No*, which features Rolf Harris with a group of children of junior age. *Beyond the Scare* (another Rolf Harris video), made in association with the Tavistock Clinic, helps teachers to examine the issues around child sexual abuse and demonstrates teacher-training sessions involving parents and teachers. These are available from The Tavistock Clinic, 43 Drury Lane, London WC2B 5RT.

The pack designed by Ann Peake, *Working with Sexually Abused Children*, comprises two story books; a colouring book; a series of practice papers for professionals concerning, for example, communicating with children and young people, counselling children, planning and organising group work for older children. It is a most attractive, informative and practical pack and is available from The Children's Society, Marjery Street, London WC1X 0JL.

Keeping Safe is a practical guide on talking to children by Michelle Elliott (1988), a teacher and educational psychologist, who is on the Advisory Council of the NSPCC and Childline. This book is an excellent one for teachers and parents alike. It presents, in a simple, straightforward style, suggestions for teaching children how to keep safe.

Where there is a clear school policy approved by teachers, governors and parents together on sex education, including safety teaching, the teacher will feel confident to tackle this difficult but important area of the curriculum in ways which suit his or her particular talent and the age group concerned. If such a policy does not exist it is imperative that discussions are initiated and policies worked on as soon as senior staff can be given the impetus to do so.

Conclusion

In this chapter the most contentious area of EBD, child abuse, has been examined briefly from the point of view of the teacher. Child physical abuse and neglect, as well as all forms of sexual abuse, bring with them an added abuse – emotional abuse. Knowledge of their existence also constitutes a form of abuse to the concerned adult forced to recognise that they do exist.

It would be short-sighted, however, to conclude this chapter on child abuse without mentioning the very real feelings of trepidation which teachers, as others in the caring professions, rightly feel when dealing with children they suspect or know to have been abused. The child's special need is to build a genuine adult-child relationship, in which there is enough trust for him to express primitive and disturbed feelings and behaviour. Male teachers in particular may feel very inhibited about showing affection to a pupil with these needs, especially if that pupil is reacting to the abuse by being sexually precocious. In practice, the concerned and informed teacher will strike a balance between taking constructive 'calculated' risks in allowing disturbed children to form close therapeutic relationships with them and avoiding what could be compromising situations.

The necessity for a whole school policy with built-in support for all members of staff is clearly essential if teachers are to fulfil their potential positive role in helping to prevent abuse in all its distressing forms through an imaginative use of the curriculum; in learning how to recognise and respond to warning signals about abuse, which children are sending out; in handling disclosures and their aftermath with sensitivity and a clear sense of direction; in keeping, at all times, the child's best interests at the heart of any intervention.

Teachers, because of their daily close contact with children and the experience they gain in communicating with them, are consciously or unconsciously guiding their emotional and social as well as intellectual development. They should grasp the nettle of seeking to help the abused child firmly and be prepared to take their rightful place in the Area Child Protection Team when one of their pupils is involved in any form of abuse, be it neglect, physical, sexual, or emotional abuse.

CHAPTER NINE

Conduct Disorders

Introduction

Within the teaching profession there has always been an acknowledgement that, without control of the class, it is impossible to teach. When the Secretary of State for Education announced that there was to be an enquiry into discipline (The Elton Report, 1989) he pointed out that education was dependent on good order. Whether we seek to control through good relationships with pupils or through a more authoritarian, rule-based approach, few teachers would argue that the feeling of being in control of one's pupils and classroom is essential.

Children who pose a threat to this control, therefore, form one of the most recognised and disturbing categories of EBD – the children coming under Quay's category of Conduct Disorder (see Chapter One). They are the children who externalise their problems and cause as much, if not more, disturbance to those in daily contact with them than to themselves. These children are impossible to ignore in school and their behaviours, if not their real problems, are rarely overlooked.

In this chapter, conduct disorders generally will be discussed briefly and then examined in more detail under the sub-headings of aggression, disruption, juvenile delinquency and bullying.

Defining conduct disorders

According to the DSM 111 (1980), these disorders involve a repetitive and persistent pattern of conduct in which either:

- the basic rights of others are violated, or
- major age-appropriate social norms or rules are violated.

Four major types of conduct disorders are described, the specific diagnosis depending on (a) the degree to which the child shows adequate social relationships, and (b) the presence or absence of aggressive, anti-social behaviour. The four types are:

(1) Under-socialised aggressive
(2) Under-socialised non-aggressive
(3) Socialised aggressive
(4) Socialised non-aggressive

As Herbert (1982) points out, the common theme running through all four sub-types is anti-social disruptiveness and the social disapproval the children earn for flouting society's rules. Their behaviour is always disturbing and often harmful to others. The child with a socialised conduct disorder does have friends and can become attached to others, whereas the non-socialised child is often a loner. The aggressive-conduct disordered child is physically violent and his behaviours can include vandalism, fire setting, mugging and theft outside the house, involving confrontation with the victim. The non-aggressive conduct disordered child violates important rules, for instance he truants, runs away from home, abuses drugs, lies and steals but without confronting the victim.

Among childhood problems anti-social behaviours rank relatively high but the true incidence is hard to establish as the children are such an heterogeneous group. The Isle of Wight Study (Rutter *et al.*, 1975) found that of the sample of children. aged from 10 to 11 from a rural area, 4 per cent showed symptoms of conduct disorder. This was almost doubled in the sample of children from an urban area of London. Boys have consistently been found to be more anti-social than girls. Graham (1979) found conduct disorder to be three times more prevalent in boys than girls, and the onset appeared to be much later in girls.

Aggression in children

Researchers for the Elton Report (DES, 1989) found that about one in two hundred teachers in secondary schools had been subjected to incidents of a clearly violent nature in the week under review. One headteacher, for instance, was threatened by a boy with a pickaxe handle and soon afterwards had to confront a girl who had brought a machete to school 'to sort somebody out'. Although these incidents of real violence are comparatively rare they are very disturbing when they do take place and teachers feel the need to be prepared with some understanding of violent behaviour in case it occurs in their class.

The word 'violence' in this context is used to describe the physical expression of aggression. Aggression itself need not always show itself physically, though when verbally 'battered' by someone, we do feel and say that we have been 'attacked'.

Theories to account for the presence of aggression vary. Freud (1933) considered aggression to be one of the two basic instincts with which we are born — the other being sex. The psycho-analytic school (Storr, 1970) sees the aggressive instinct as positive in that it fuels the drive for independence and survival, but negative when the individual has not come to terms with this drive and either turns the aggression inwards or expresses it in childish, explosive forms against others. Lorenz (1966) gives an ethological explanation for aggression drawn from analogies taken from all animal species who, according to Lorenz, have an in-born *need* to aggress. It is part of the life-preserving organisation of instincts, but in humans, though basically constructive, it can become distorted. The behaviourists (Bandura, 1973) maintain that aggressive behaviour, like all behaviour, is learned, especially through modelling.

Whatever theory, or synthesis of theories, we favour, we are often aware that possible violent reactions lie near the surface in some of our pupils and that it is part of our 'civilising' task as teachers to prevent violence, aggression and cruelty in children as portrayed for example by William Golding in *Lord of the Flies*. As part of our lesson planning we can seek to channel aggressive energy into non-harmful activities, such as competitive sports or intellectual debate. In the way we talk and relate respectfully to children and by creating a healthily disciplined environment in which they can learn, we can model non-aggressive strategies for the constructive use of power, authority and influence.

Many variables identified with destructive aggression have been identified, including low family income, large family, marital discord, parent criminal behaviour (Farrington, 1978). However, children of parents who remain together, but quarrel continuously, are as likely to be as aggressive as some children whose parents separate (Robins,1966). Individual temperament becomes an important variable. Harsh parental discipline with the use of punishment, especially corporal punishment, has been shown to produce aggressive behaviour in children (Farrington, 1978), but inconsistent handling, for example where mother is permissive and father is restrictive, is rather more damaging (Hetherington and Martin, 1979).

The most common and effective approach to modifying aggressive behaviour is to use the behavioural procedure of operant conditioning by positive reinforcement of non-aggressive behaviour. Grieger, Kauffman and Grieger (1976) give the interesting example of a positive reinforcement programme in which the major reinforcer was peer praise. The teacher of a class of young children asked them to report the 'friendly' behaviours of classmates after base-line observations of co-operative and aggressive behaviours in class had been taken. The children identified as 'friendly' were given a badge with a happy face on it. In the next stage of the experiment the children were asked to report 'unfriendly' acts, instead of 'friendly' acts. No specific punishment was provided. In the final stage 'friendly' acts were again reported by the children but at this point no happy badges were given. The results showed that when peer attention and praise were provided (Report + Happy Face and Report Only phases) aggressive behaviour decreased markedly. When 'unfriendly' behaviour was reported, aggressive behaviour returned to base-line levels.

In the Elton Report (DES, 1989) it was found that primary school teachers' experiences were different from their secondary school colleagues in that more than seven out of ten primary staff reported having to deal with physical aggression towards other pupils at least once during the week with about four in ten in secondary school staff. Perhaps junior school teachers' attempts to 'civilise' their pupils have paid off!

In order to help teachers feel that, on those rare occasions when they are violently assaulted, they are not alone, the Elton Committee recommended that Chief Police Officers and Crown prosecutors should take staff morale seriously, as a matter of public interest, when deciding whether or not to prosecute in cases of assault against teachers, and that those assaulted should be entitled to compensation.

Disruption

Although significant, incidents of physical aggression are exceptional. Elton found that the main worry of teachers was of being

Figure 9.1 Disruptive behaviours reported by secondary teachers in the classroom the previous week

Type of pupil behaviour (listed by frequency of occurrence)	Reported frequency	
	At least once during week (%)	At least daily (%)
Talking out of turn (e.g. by making remarks, calling out, distracting others by chattering)	97	53
Calculated idleness or work avoidance (e.g. delaying start to work set, not having essential books or equipment)	87	25
Hindering other pupils (e.g. by distracting them from work, interfering with equipment or materials)	86	26
Not being punctual (e.g. being late to school or lessons)	82	17
Making unnecessary (non-verbal) noise (e.g. by scraping chairs, banging objects, moving clumsily)	77	25
Persistently infringing class (or school) rules (e.g. on dress, pupil behaviour)	68	17
Getting out of seat without permission	62	14
Verbal abuse towards other pupils (e.g. offensive or insulting remarks)	62	10
General rowdiness, horseplay or mucking about	61	10
Cheeky or impertinent remarks or responses	58	10
Physical aggression towards other pupils (e.g. by pushing, punching, striking)	42	6
Verbal abuse towards teacher (e.g. offensive, insulting, insolent or threatening remarks)	15	1
Physical destructiveness (e.g. breaking objects, damaging furniture and fabric)	14	1
Physical aggression towards teacher	1.7	0

worn down by a 'continuous stream of relatively minor disruptions'. (See Figure 9.1 for the Elton analysis of the range of disruptive behaviours encountered by teachers.)

Teachers' evidence to Elton showed that discipline problems were 'serious' where they also reported a higher proportion of pupils below average ability, or higher proportions coming from deprived areas. Teachers were a little more likely to report problems if they had more pupils from the inner cities or, interestingly, if their school had made greater use of corporal punishment around the time when it was formally abolished.

Definitions of disruption, in itself an educational 'in word' of the 1980s, centre mainly around the effect of pupils' behaviour on the teacher. The use of the word is undoubtedly a comment about the teacher's feeling of having lost authority. This will have a great deal to do with the individual teacher's concept of what constitutes acceptable and non-acceptable behaviour and also to do with the type of lesson involved. For example, a drama teacher, or creative English teacher may wish pupils to discuss ideas amongst themselves, use their initiative and show some degree of uninhibited behaviour. Another teacher of a more formally taught subject, may demand silence, total lack of movement about the classroom and no use of pupil initiative. A pupil who is naturally effervescent and extrovert could appear co-operative in one situation and disruptive in the other. Whole schools also vary in the boundaries to pupil behaviour which they set. Children who are not considered disruptive in one school, where allowances are made for sub-cultural differences and formal rules are at a minimum, might be considered disruptive in another more 'traditional' school.

Problems of control and managing disruptive pupils are particularly difficult for inexperienced teachers. The mentor system operated in some schools to support new teachers would seem an ideal way of helping young teachers to learn from, and model on, the effective classroom management styles of more experienced teachers.

The Elton Committee concluded that the problem of disruption could be reduced by helping teachers to become better managers. There is some concern, however, (Hanko, 1989) that training in management skills, whilst it *may* be effective in setting necessary limits to unacceptable behaviour, does not always deepen the teacher's understanding of the special emotional needs the disruptive behaviour may be expressing.

The Education Reform Act also reinforces this lack of need, on the part of the teacher, to understand as well as to manage the disruptive child. The DES Circular No.5, in stating that Heads may start temporary exemption from the National Curriculum procedures to come into effect more quickly in cases of *disruptive pupils* (i.e. in less than a month) is implying that these pupils do not have emotional and behavioural difficulties which are either (a) exacerbated by contributory features within school, or (b) open to remediation within normal school practice if the needs are rightly diagnosed.

In order to understand the individual disruptive child's special educational needs we should be prepared to look at factors within the child himself and his family system and factors within the classroom and school. Lawrence *et al.*, (1984) in their research into 'disruptive children – disruptive schools', asked staff of a multi-racial, co-educational, urban comprehensive school to offer explanations of pupils' disruptive behaviour. Amongst the factors concerned with the child himself were:

- Has a bad temper – needs little provocation
- Lacks intelligence and reasoning ability
- Is deprived/disadvantaged at home
- Is boisterous in response to being controlled
- Is emotionally disturbed
- Is an under-achiever for his potential
- Has real learning difficulties
- Comes from a mixed race parentage
- Is affected, particularly if West Indian, by racial prejudice.

Some factors which were more related to the possibility of teachers' ability to meet a disruptive child's needs in school were:

- Needs to feel a person of worth
- Needs to be helped with learning difficulties, especially reading
- Needs lessons which do not bore him
- Sometimes a lonely child who desperately needs attention so seeks it through being disruptive
- Sees no point in working because he faces unemployment when he leaves school as he will have no qualifications
- Does not know the teacher – either because the teacher is a supply teacher, a new member of staff or simply does not teach the child.

The 'bad chemistry' of the classroom was mentioned by some staff, the coming together of certain children with certain staff whose personalities are incompatible, as a possible trigger for disruptive behaviour.

The question of how much a school reflects the value system of the teacher as opposed to pupils has been discussed in relation to truancy but is equally relevant to a discussion on disruption – as is the question of relevant curriculum. In to-day's climate, whilst acknowledging that individual disruptive children may have personal or pathological reasons for their disturbing behaviour, we are starting to look at what can be done within the school itself to alleviate the problem for teachers and children alike.

The strategies employed by secondary teachers, as reported to Elton (see Figure 9.2) reflect a moderate and reasoning approach on the part of most staff. The most extreme form of action, exclusion from school, is sometimes related to psychiatric disorders in excluded pupils and their families (York *et al.*, 1972). This is not, however, always the case. Galloway *et al.* (1985) in their study of Sheffield schools noted strong evidence for the importance of school variables in determining exclusion rates. Five out of the 39 schools surveyed accounted for more than 50 per cent of excluded pupils over a three-year period. They concluded that policies on exclusion were idiosyncratic to each school with the way in which pastoral care was practised, as opposed to its formal organisation, as a possible variable.

McManus (1989) in a similar survey of 49 schools found that the procedures used by a school might, unintentionally, escalate minor problems into major confrontations in which the authority of the school may be perceived to be at stake, thus promoting drastic action. Negative referrals to senior staff were found to be particularly alarmist in their consequences yet, as Elton emphasised, teachers need to be able to confide their anxieties in seniors and receive support from them. These support systems should also aim to *increase* rather than decrease teachers' ability to find their *own* solutions to problems they face in their classroom.

Exclusion of a pupil, though it may solve an immediate crisis, is not attempting to address the real needs of the pupil or the problems of the teacher and should only be used as a last resort. The effects can be long-term and far-reaching. In Britain, for example, school reports influence magistrates' sentencing policies and children who have been excluded or suspended from school are twice as likely to receive custodial sentences (Graham, 1988).

For some children, however, a period of suspension for involvement in severe continuous disruptive behaviour and classroom confrontation has proved useful. In the Sheffield study Galloway discovered that when pupils were suspended from school and then taught in 'special groups' it was a valuable experience because:

- It provided a cooling off period for staff and child before drastic action was taken.

Figure 9.2 The strategies and sanctions secondary teachers were employing to deal with difficult classes or pupils and their perceived effectiveness

Type of strategy or sanction	Teachers reporting recent use:		Perceived effectiveness (of strategies used)		
	At least once (%)	Often or quite often (%)	Most effective (%)	Most ineffective (%)	
Reasoning with a pupil or pupils in the classroom setting	92	55	21	12	(of 2281)*
Reasoning with a pupil or pupils outside the classroom setting	89	46	32	2	(of 2194)
Requiring pupil or pupils to do 'extra work' of some sort	76	23	8	10	(of 1871)
Deliberately ignoring minor disruptions or infringements	71	19	3	10	(of 1755)
Keeping a pupil or pupils in (i.e. detention)	67	17	15	7	(of 1645)
Discussing with the whole class why things are going wrong	66	21	9	10	(of 1626)
Asking pupil to withdraw temporarily from the room or class	61	11	13	5	(of 1500)
Referring a pupil or pupils to another teacher	50	7	7	4	(of 1237)
Removing privileges	44	9	5	7	(of 1064)
Sending a pupil or pupils direct to the head, deputy or another senior teacher	27	2	14	6	(of 753)
Requesting suspension from school	9	0	0	5	(of 224)

*The figures should be interpreted as follows. Of those teachers (2281 in all) who reported that they had used this particular strategy recently, 21% said it was the 'most effective' strategy they had used while 12% said it was the 'most ineffective'.

- It gave an opportunity for any stresses within the home to be investigated.
- It provided the opportunity to look at any precipitating stresses within the school.

The separate special unit for disruptive pupils, so popular in the 1970s (in 1977 there were 239 units in 69 local authorities and by 1980 the number had risen by 100, collectively providing places for 6,791 pupils) emphasised the segregation of disruptive pupils from mainstream education. Following the 1981 Education Act there was a requirement to integrate children with special educational needs, including disruptive pupils, into mainstream education. The response to this was, in many cases, to compromise by having partial integration of these pupils. Special centres or withdrawal groups within mainstream schools were sometimes used. Support teachers might be appointed to support the mainstream teacher and the SEN pupil within the classroom or to withdraw such a pupil for individual tuition.

Since the implementation of the ERA and the advent of Local Management of Schools there appears to be less investment in special units for disruptive children and, sadly, reduction in the resources allocated to supporting staff in mainstream who are striving to integrate these demanding children. The teacher is thrown back once again on his personal understanding of, and empathy for, the EBD child who, in this case, is showing his disturbance through unendearing, anti-social behaviour.

General principles of good classroom management need to be applied even more stringently when dealing with disruptive pupils. Keeping the children busy and varying the activities so they do not get bored; making sure that rules are as few as possible and are both clear and enforceable, preferably having been discussed and agreed with the pupils; imaginative and stimulating use of the physical environment and seating within the classroom.

Sometimes, no matter how skilful and organised the teacher, conflict and confrontation with a pupil is inevitable. Laslett and Smith (1984) suggest that such confrontation may be beneficial where a teacher has a sound relationship with the pupil, based on a history of patience and tolerance. The confrontation may prove to be the turning point at which the pupil starts to take some responsibility for his own behaviour.

Where confrontation is unlooked for and threatens the teacher with lack of control, McManus (1989) provides some excellent guidelines as follows:

(1) *Avoid being manipulated*
   Do not fall into a reflex, angry reaction when provoked by the potentially confronting child who wishes you to do so. To avoid this, the teacher needs to be aware of his feelings of personal hurt

that both his authority as a teacher and his attempts at reason-ableness are being attacked. It is also tempting to play to the audience of the other children and to the potential audience of senior colleagues who may enter at any moment. The emotional needs of the disruptive pupil will then not be perceived or responded to and the confrontation is likely to escalate with everyone eventually losing face.

(2) *Try to identify the pupil's point of view*
This is another occasion for possibly attempting to 'reframe the problem', especially if the child is one with whom the teacher normally has a warm relationship. The very closeness of the relationship can trigger anger, for instance, which the child feels in relation to a parent and this may in fact be a positive and necessary expression of ambivalence as far as the child is concerned and a step towards his resolution of an inner conflict.

(3) *Avoid ratchet statements*
A ratchet can usually only turn one way at a time. In this context such a statement refers to any threat that cannot be carried out or to any hurtful remark that cannot be withdrawn. Such actions only raise the temperature of any conflict and should not be made.

(4) *Accept or divert an attack*
As McManus says, it sometimes costs nothing in terms of esteem or control, simply to accept an insult or act of defiance, especially if it can be diverted into a humorous sally. Robbie Laslett quotes, in lectures, his own experience of being called a fat, ugly, bastard by one confronting pupil. 'Not so much about the fat!' he retorted, with a smile, and the confrontation evaporated in the ensuing laughter!

(5) *Repair the relationship*
If a confrontation has occurred and there is bitterness on both sides, the teacher should try to see the pupil alone before the next time-tabled meeting when the rest of the class will be waiting with baited breath for another instalment of the drama. It is not demeaning for the teacher to lead the way in apologising, and the respect shown to the pupil through this may achieve a breakthrough that no amount of 'discipline' could achieve. Most confrontational pupils come from backgrounds where they are not secure in the acceptance and love of adults and a teacher who can recognise and meet the need this child has, in spite of his unattractive behaviour, is truly fulfilling his pastoral role.

Figure 9.3 Recommendations of the Elton Committee

● Headteachers and teachers should in consultation with governors, develop whole-school behaviour policies which are clearly understood by pupils, parents and other school staff.

● Schools should ensure that their rules are derived from the principles underlying their behaviour policies and are consistent with them.

● Schools should strike a healthy balance between rewards and punishments. Both should be clearly specified.

● Headteachers and teachers should avoid the punishment of whole groups.

● Headteachers and teachers should avoid punishments which humiliate pupils.

● Headteachers and staff should: be alert to signs of bullying and racial harassment; deal firmly with all such behaviour; take action based on clear rules which are backed by appropriate sanctions and systems to protect and support victims.

● Schools should not use rigid streaming arrangements to group their pupils by ability.

● Headteachers and staff should adopt comprehensive policies for the care of premises, with responsibilities allocated to specific people, including pupils.

● LEAs and governing bodies with responsibility for buildings should help schools to create a better environment for both staff and pupils by providing soft-floor coverings and other noise-reducing features wherever possible.

● LEAs and governing bodies which employ school staff should ensure that midday supervisors are given adequate training in the management of pupils' behaviour.

In their final report, the Elton Committee made many recommendations, some of which are shown in Figure 9.3. The emphasis on a 'whole school policy' is a common theme when trying to identify and meet the special educational needs of children and never more so than in the case of children with emotional and behavioural difficulties. The teacher, particularly in mainstream, who is genuinely trying to meet the needs of demanding EBD children within a busy classroom, needs the security and confidence which a positive 'whole school' approach can start to give.

Hanko (1989) advocates the use of joint problem-solving work-shops, to be held on a regular basis within schools, and which could pool the existing knowledge and expertise concerning children with EBD and help to meet both the short and long term needs of the teacher. Ideally these would be led by an expert consultant whose job would be not only to generate information that would be helpful to a case under discussion, but also to discover and build on the teachers' strengths, helping them to ask the relevant questions about the child and to build up confidence in their own ability to find solutions to problems.

The identification of the teacher as creator, at least in part, of his difficulties with disruptive children is a fairly recent phenomenon. In general, until Rutter *et al.* (1975) began their investigations the teacher was seen to be the victim of the aggressive/disruptive child and in no way the protagonist. The Plowden Report (DES, 1967), for example, defined disruptive behaviour in terms of pupil or family deficits related to social factors. The Elton Report has helped us to see that we play an *active* part in our pupils' behaviour or mis-behaviour. Even with a well defined 'whole school approach' our perception of our role and our personal value system will play a large part in the behaviour we elicit from our pupils. If we can reframe the problem of disruption to see it from the pupil's point of view, we may find that some of the demands of our school 'system' are unreasonable and could be modified to accommodate potentially disruptive children. Alternatively, if the disruptive child does not have the skills to meet the reasonable demands of the school system, it is our job to create a climate of tolerance, humour and respect in which this objective can be realised.

Juvenile delinquency

Historically the notion of juvenile delinquency, as a form of conduct disorder, was created by the initiation of Juvenile Courts at the end of the 1880s. Subsequent legislation created a mixed model of legal and social treatment approaches to delinquent behaviour which exists to this day.

The term 'delinquency' is a legal one and is used to refer to a juvenile (usually under 18), who has committed an act that would be considered criminal in an adult. This definition covers a wide range of behaviours from graffiti drawings to homicide, and the emotional and behavioural disturbances and needs of this group of children who are labelled delinquent vary considerably. For example, one child may steal because he has little conscience or guilt about taking something which does not belong to him; another child who has run away from home to avoid sexual abuse may steal food or money to stay alive; a third child might be a member of a gang, the members of which view 'stealing' as a fun activity; yet another child may steal because he comes from a family and sub-culture where stealing is 'normal' and the only crime is to be found out.

Quay (1964), investigating the possibility that identifiable sub-types of delinquency might exist, factor-analysed the data from 115 institutionalised male delinquents and arrived at four clusters of inter-related behavioural characteristics as follows:

(1) *Socialised subcultural delinquency*
Has bad companions, stays out late at night, is accepted by a delinquent sub-group and has strong allegiance to peers; is low on shyness and seclusiveness. Can be thought of as a relatively normal individual, whose delinquent behaviour relates to interaction with a delinquent sub-group.

(2) *Unsocialised psychopathic delinquency*
Does not participate in gang activities and is not acceptable to a delinquent sub-group. Is delinquent in defiance of authority, assaultive, irritable, impudent, verbally aggressive, feels persecuted but has no ability to respond either to punishment or to praise. Is mistrustful, displays inadequate guilt feelings and seeks out trouble.

(3) *Disturbed neurotic delinquency*
Generally unhappy, timid, shy and withdrawn, prone to worry and displays guilt and anxiety over his behaviour. Physical complaints may be quite prominent. Less aggressive, more accepting of authority and more amenable to change than children types (1) and (2). Delinquent behaviour is secondary to emotional problems.

(4) *Inadequate immature delinquency*
Tends to be easily frustrated, picked on by others, passive and pre-occupied and usually not accepted by delinquent peers. Rather than having major psychological problems, he appears to have a poorly developed behavioural repertoire. Is generally inadequate in his functioning and unable to cope with the demands of normal environments and systems.

As there is no one definition or description of juvenile delinquency so there is no single theory as to its aetiology. The sociological view expressed, for example, by Cloward and Ohlin (1969) focuses on the child's inability to reach socially valued goals. Other sociologists associate delinquency with sub-cultural norms (Shaw and McKay, 1969). The psycho-dynamic view blames faulty early relationships with parents and suggests that the delinquent is either seeking punishment to atone for guilt or, because of unresolved anger, is seeking to hurt someone. The behavioural psychologists would say the delinquency is learned behaviour modelled on family patterns of behaviour.

There is much support for the genetic hypothesis of delinquency (Cadonet, 1978) but Rutter (1972) argues that delinquent behaviour as such is not inherited, though inherited temperamental differences, in conjunction with family discord and disruption, may predispose a child to become delinquent. It is also maintained that chromosomal abnormalities may contribute to anti-social behaviour. In 1961 Sandberg *et al.* discovered the XYY syndrome in which some males have an extra Y chromosome. These males were found to be overly represented in mental and penal institutions. A relationship between XYY syndrome and childhood emotional problems, including delinquency, was found by Ratcliff and Field (1982).

Farley (1973) proposed an arousal/sensation-seeking model of delinquency in which children born with arousal deficits seek out novel, exciting activities, like delinquency, to attain some level of stimulation. These are the delinquents whom Quay characterised as psychopathic, pathological stimulation seekers.

When it comes to examining the socio-economic backgrounds of delinquents, it is often assumed that the majority come from poor families. It is difficult to establish, however, whether the findings, based on official delinquency rates, reflect the actual degree of delinquency from various socio-economic backgrounds, or whether they relate more to the prevailing law enforcement practices. Self-report studies, however, such as Gold and Petronio (1980), have found little in the way of a relationship between poor economic background and delinquency. Children from all social classes admit involvement in illegal practices.

Family variables *have* proved to be significant in many studies, e.g. Moore and Arthur (1983). Parents of delinquents have been found generally to display lower levels of moral judgment, to be more extreme in terms of discipline – very permissive or very strict – to be more hostile and rejecting and to be more likely to use physical punishment.

For the teacher, the hypotheses linking delinquency with learning disabilities are of particular interest. There is no clear evidence that learning difficulties per se *cause* delinquent behaviour but there is a great deal of evidence that many delinquent children *have* learning difficulties – see, for example, Lane (1980). Anti-social behaviour may be the result of a child's frustration and humiliation in not being able to achieve academically in step with his peers or, because the child is suffering from a conduct disorder, he may not be able to realise his academic potential. Whatever the reality of this chicken and egg situation, the child clearly has a need to be helped with his learning difficulty and when this is achieved some delinquent children give up their anti-social behaviour.

As already stated, there are many types of delinquency and the first task of the teacher, who wishes to make a constructive contribution to the child's wider educational needs, is to make an assessment as to which sub-group a particular pupil belongs. Let us return for a moment to Quay's four major categories:

The socialised subcultural delinquent.

This child is not suffering from emotional disturbance or social isolation and is usually quite happy with his place in the family system and life in general. His delinquency is part of 'fun gang activity' and should be dealt with as such. Clearly, the child and his delinquent peers need to learn that it is not 'having fun' which is unacceptable but the interference in other peoples' rights. A straightforward programme of behaviour modification in which the child is rewarded heavily for both educational progress and acceptable behaviour, particularly if the programme involves his delinquent peers, can produce relatively rapid results. Unfortunately, if this type of intervention is not undertaken, this particular delinquent is likely to finish up in an institution exclusively for delinquents, where the chances are his predisposition for delinquency will be reinforced by the peer group. Recidivism rates for many such institutions suggest that 70 per cent to 80 per cent of boys are likely to be re-arrested within a year of their release.

An alternative legal option to deal with such a delinquent is for the court to impose a supervision order. For younger children the supervision will usually be carried out by a social worker and for older children by a probation officer. The success of this approach will depend largely on the quality of the supervisor's help but the teacher is in a position both to monitor the child's commitment to the goals of the supervision and to support both child and supervisor.

The unsocialised psychopathic delinquent.

These children, though few in number, form the most difficult group of delinquents to help. Their inability to profit from either punishment or praise, their need to seek out trouble and their complete lack of conscience or remorse, are not endearing features and, in fact, they appear to have no need of our help or our approval. We will need the support of the child psychological and psychiatric services to even contain a child in this category and, sadly, the prognosis for future good mental health is poor. We are likely to have to face defeat in 'curing' the truly psychopathic delinquent and should prepare ourselves for this by being realistic about our chances for success.

The disturbed neurotic delinquent.

If the teacher has rightly picked up that this child's delinquency is associated with unhappiness and an unmet emotional need, his next task is to try to surface that need. These children, because of their ability to feel anxiety and guilt over their delinquent behaviour, are *relatively* easy to help and will respond to genuine attempts to understand them. They may be the victims of some form of abuse at home, physical, sexual or emotional. They may be rejected, or feel to be rejected, by their parents and are often desperately insecure about their future. As they do have a capacity to trust, the teacher should build on this and, through a counselling relationship, help the child to come to terms with his fears and anxieties. There may be a need for help from outside school, for example group or family therapy, or support for an over-burdened mother from a Family Service Unit.

The inadequate immature delinquent.

These children resort to delinquency as a poor substitute for being able to take part in their peer group social activities. They are short on social skills and, therefore, this is the area in which the teacher can provide constructive support. Improve this child's self-image first by praising consistently and frequently his efforts to achieve, both educationally and socially, and second by increasing his behavioural repertoire to enable him to exchange his delinquent behaviours for behaviours which are more acceptable and thus more rewarding to him and more self-esteem enhancing.

Bullying

For many years bullying was accepted as almost a 'normal' feature of school life and, particularly in relation to boys, was seen as something with which a child should learn to cope on his own as its occurrence is of no great significance. More recently, however, the effects of childhood bullying have been seen sometimes to have life-long implications. A two-year study by Kidscape involving 4,000 children found that 8 per cent of the sample had become so disturbed by bullying that they had run away from home, refused to go to school, or even attempted suicide. The effect on bullies themselves can equally be lasting. Robins (1978), in a 30-year follow up study, found that aggressive behaviour in children over the age of eight continued throughout their lives, manifesting itself in criminality, violent behaviour, marital difficulties and psychiatric illness.

Definitions of the term 'bullying' vary in order to cover a wide field encompassing physical and psychological bullying, name-calling and teasing, jostling and punching, intimidation and extortion, assault, maiming and murder. Askew (1989) defines bullying briefly as 'the wilful, conscious desire to hurt another'.

Teachers are no longer perceiving bullying as an insignificant problem and are starting to look at both the bully and the victim as showing signs of emotional and behavioural disturbance. They are also becoming aware that bullying is more widespread than had been formerly assessed. In a recent survey of 783 seven- to 13-year olds, O'Moore (1989), found that teachers vastly underestimated the incidence of bullying in their schools. Less than a quarter of the number of bullies were identified by them and awareness of the number of victims was only marginally higher.

Significant bullying is more prevalent at primary level: 11 per cent of primary school children experience repeated bullying as opposed to half that number in secondary schools (Olweus, 1984). Roland (1988) discovered twice as many victims amongst boys as amongst girls and three times more boy bullies than girl bullies. Roland maintained that just as many girls are both victims and bullies but the nature of the bullying is more subtle and therefore less observed.

Tattum (1989) divides bullying into two broad categories — physical and psychological. Boys are mainly associated with physical abuse, whereas psychological, verbal abuse, with the intention of isolating the victim from her peer group, is mainly associated with girls. Another insidious form of bullying is racial harassment, which as O'Moore states is often given too little attention.

As at least 15 per cent of school children are known to be bullied, and this may be just the tip of the ice-berg, it is no longer a problem to be brushed aside by the teaching profession. It is important, therefore, for us to seek some understanding of both the child bully and the child victim, so that we may take effective preventive and curative measures to reduce the amount of bullying in our schools.

Stephenson and Smith (1989), in their Cleveland study, identified three different types of bully whom they called:

- The **strong bully** — physically strong, active and assertive, derives pleasure from aggressive incident, fairly popular with peers.
- The **anxious bully** — less popular and less confident, more problems at home and poor academically.
- The **bully/victim** — children who were both bullies and victims and found to be the least popular of all the groups. They were physically stronger than their victims, easily provoked and also very provocative.

By contrast, the children who become victims are usually seen, and indeed see themselves, as detached, critical, aloof and shy, serious and very sensitive to threats (Byrne, 1978). They are generally weaker than other pupils, less intelligent, poor attainers and suffer from low self-esteem. Sometimes the victim seems to invite bullying, for example the bully/victim who actively provokes and the 'willing victim' (Wolfson, 1989), who seeks attention through punishment from either teachers or peers.

Many of the factors in a child's family background which have been seen to be associated with other forms of conduct disorder apply also to the bully. Stephenson and Smith (1989) found that children who bullied were likely to come from families where there was lack of firm and consistent discipline, poor marital and child/parent relationships, financial and social problems and parents who themselves were bullies.

Having accepted that bullying in school is much more widespread than formerly acknowledged, what steps can the teacher take to reduce it and start to meet the special needs of both the victim and the bully?

We remind ourselves firstly of the need for a 'whole school policy' and commitment to that policy by a staff who create an ethos of caring. Pupils and staff also need to learn, if this does not already happen, to respect each other so that children from an early age can learn appropriate ways of responding to behaviour that is provocative. As Chazan (1989) advocates, it is not too early to start this in the infant school. If styles of discipline which are just and non-aggressive are common practice, placing more emphasis on rewards

158

than punishment, staff will be modelling a non-bullying form of authority and will be in a strong position to create a school value system in which the bullying of the weak by the strong is totally unacceptable.

Campaigns within school against bullying, such as one which aimed at strengthening teachers' relationships with pupils by meeting with victims, bullies and parents after a particular incident, can be highly effective, especially in secondary schools, from the evidence of the research.

Many victims are, of course, too afraid of the bully to break the code of secrecy which exists amongst pupils about bullying and therefore teachers need to have a clear and known commitment to taking the incidents of bullying seriously when they do come to light. In order to have the courage to tell, the victim needs to know that (a) he will be believed, and (b) that steps will be taken to protect him from further bullying. Arora (1989) suggests that the following steps should be followed when dealing with an incident:

(1) Be available to the victim with immediate sympathy and support.
(2) Treat the information seriously.
(3) Record the information precisely.
(4) Avoid dealing with the bully by using aggressive methods.
(5) Use a positive teaching approach by teaching the bully less harmful ways of achieving social dominance, for example asking him to organise an inter-form match, quiz or debate.
(6) Involve parents on the basis that bullies often have bullying parents and ask them to play a role in school, e.g.organising a school jumble sale.
(7) Ensure that there is a follow up to show that the situation is being taken seriously and the bully's behaviour is still being monitored.

The use of 'bully courts' as advocated by Laslett (1980) at which pupils, supervised by teachers, discuss and adjudicate complaints of bullying brought by children can start to involve the whole of the school's population and so reinforce a whole school policy.

Curricular work can be one of the most effective ways of dealing with bullying and there are now many projects and aids to teachers on the market. Trentham Books can supply *Sticks and stones*, a Central ITV video containing advice to teachers, children and parents, issued with a free Kidscape pack; *Only Playing Miss!* by the Neti Neti Theatre company is a powerful play that probes deeply into school bullying; and *The Trouble with Tom*, a Central ITV video for 8–12 year olds.

Besag's whole school approach (1989) suggests the use in class of videos, booklets, posters and projects designed by the teachers and pupils themselves. Role-play in which bullies and victims exchange roles and creative brain-storming sessions about bullying with all the children in the class, can help to create awareness of the emotional as well as the physical fear aroused by bullying.

A nation-wide campaign conducted in Norway and reported by Olweus (1984) proved so successful in reducing the extent of bullying that there has recently been considerable pressure to conduct a similar campaign in this country. A DES project, led by Dr Peter Smith of Sheffield University, is the long awaited first step towards a national initiative. The schools in the sample, 20 Sheffield schools, will formulate their own anti-bullying policy and intervention strategies which will be monitored for about 15 months and then assessed.

If we are prepared to see bullying as the outside sign of a special need in both the victim and the bully we should, through the imaginative use of the curriculum and the pastoral care system, be able to make some progress in reducing its harmful presence in our schools.

Conclusion

In this chapter the wide field of conduct disorders has been discussed with the knowledge that children in this group have caused much stress and heartache to teachers struggling to meet the valid educational and social needs of all the pupils in their class. A need for mutual support and pooling of expertise and resources in order to help this EBD child, without destroying the teachers's feeling of being in control, has been underlined. Whole school policies and national policies, as defined by Elton, constitute a vital foundation for the concerned teacher, but nothing can replace the individual teacher's capacity to relate to these most difficult pupils with respect, affection and humour – even though, on a bad day, they may drive us to despair – if not to drink!

Conclusions

The world of the emotionally disturbed child is bewildering, insecure, often hostile and sometimes very lonely. As teachers we form an important part of that world. Many hours of a child's life are spent in our company and the day to day understanding and relationship we offer to a child can make all the difference to his quality of life.

EBD children are often not the most rewarding children with whom to work as, having been given so little in life, they do not have much to give. Once we can earn their trust, however, there is a deep well of untapped reserves, both intellectually and emotionally, to be explored and then the rewards for the teacher can be very real indeed.

See Me After School has tried to shed a little light on some of the vast range of disturbed and disturbing behaviours which a teacher may encounter in the course of his career, with the aim of increasing his understanding and empathy for the EBD child.

At this moment in time, April 1991, when the financial implications of the Education Reform Act are beginning to bite, a survey of local education authorities has found that the number of children with emotional and behavioural problems permanently excluded from their schools has gone up in 35 out of 60 authorities. Some schools, however, both special and mainstream, are continuing to cope with, and offer a constructive service to, these 'difficult' children.

The author would suggest that this is possible where the school — that is to say, the staff, pupils, governors and parents — are open to honest communication, genuine respect for each other, enthusiasm for the task in hand and an ability to work as a team.

The Elton Committee, like Rutter and his colleagues in a former decade, were struck by the different 'feel' or atmosphere of the schools they visited:

Our conversations with teachers left us convinced that some schools have a more positive attitude than others. This positive attitude was not related to the social or intellectual background of the children but to what went on in school.

There may always be some EBD children who need to be, if only for a short time, moved into special education, in order to have their special emotional, social and learning needs met by expert teachers in small classes.

The aim of this book, however, has been to enable all teachers to further their understanding of how the EBD child behaves and feels. Teachers have immense personal and professional resources which can be used to further the education, in its widest sense, of EBD children. With the right motivation, training and support the author is convinced that they will continue to do so, in spite of feeling at times that their best efforts are both futile and unrewarded.

The EBD child awakens in us areas of our own childhood we may feel we have left far behind but, in our efforts to make contact with these seemingly 'hopeless' children, we may find that not only do we enrich their lives but also our own.

References

Achenbach, T.M. (1966) The classification of children's psychiatric symptons: A factor analytic study. *Psychological Monographs*, 80. Whole no. 615.

Adams, P.L. (1973) *Obsessive Children*. New York: Brunner/Mazel.

Apter, Steven J. (1982) *Troubled Children, Troubled Systems*. Oxford: Pergamon.

Arora, C. (1989) Bullying – Action & Intervention. *Pastoral Care*, September 1989: 44–46.

Askew, S. (1989) Aggressive behaviour in boys. In Tattum, D. and Lane, D. (eds). *Bullying In Schools*. Stoke-on-Trent: Trentham Books.

Baher, E. *et al.* (1976) *At Risk: An Account of the Work of the Battered Child Research Department, NSPCC* London: Routledge and Kegan Paul.

Baker, A. and Duncan, S. (1985) Child Sexual Abuse. In *A study of Prevalence in Great Britain in Child Abuse and Neglect*, Vol. 9: 457–467.

Bandura, A. (1973) *Aggression: A Social Learning Analysis*. New Jersey: Prentice-Hall.

Bandura, A. (1977) *Social Learning Theory*. Englewood Cliffs, New Jersey: Prentice-Hall.

Barker, P. (1971) *Basic Child Psychiatry*. London: Granada.

Barker, R.G. and Wright, H.F. (1955) *Midwest and its children: The Psychological Ecology of an American Town*. Evanston, Ill.: Row-Peterson.

Bednar, M.J. and Haviland, D.S. (1969) *The Role of Physical Environment in the Education of Children with Learning Disabilities*. New York: Centre for Architectural Research.

Bender, B. (1976) Self-chosen victims. *Child Welfare*, LV, 6: 417–422.

Bentovim, A. (1987) *Child Sex Abuse in the U.S.A.* Unpublished paper.

Berg, I. (1980) School refusal in early adolescence. In Hersov, L. and Berg, I. (eds) *Out of School*. Chichester: John Wiley and Sons Ltd.

Besag, V. (1989) *Bullies and Victims in Schools*. Milton Keynes: Open University Press.

Bettelheim, B. (1955) *Love is not Enough*. New York: Free Press.

Bowlby, J. (1953) *Child Care and the Growth of Love*. Harmondsworth: Penguin.

Bowlby, J. (1969) *Attachment and Loss*. London: Hogarth.

Bradley, C. (1937) The behaviour of children receiving benzedrine. *American Journal of Psychiatry*, 94: 577–585.

Brennan, W.K. (1985) *Curriculum for Special Needs*. Milton Keynes: Open University Press.

Brown, K.M. (1963) *Symposium on School Refusal*. APSW.

Browne, A. and Finkelhor, D. (1986) Impact of child sexual abuse: A review of research. *Psychological Bulletin*, Vol. 99, 1.

Byrne, E. (1978) *Women and Education*. London: Tavistock.

Cadonet, R.J. (1978) Psychopathology in adopted away offspring of biologic parents with anti-social behaviour. *Archives of General Psychology*, 35: 176–184.

Cairns, R.B. (1979) *Social Development: The Origins and Plasticity of Interchanges*. San Francisco: W.H. Freeman.

Charles, J. (1983) Child Abuse: Dangerous misconceptions. *Community Care* 1 December 1983.

Charlton-Seifort, J., Stratton, B.D. and Williams, M.G. (1980). Sweet and slow: Diet can affect learning. *Academic Therapy*, 16: 211–217.

Chazan, M. (1989) Bullying in the infant school. In Tattum, D. and Lane, D. (eds) *Bullying in Schools*. Stoke-on-Trent: Trentham Books.

Chesterman, M. (1985) *Child Sexual Abuse in Social Work*. University of East Anglia Monograph.

Christopherson, E.R. and Rapoff, M.A. (1983) Toileting problems in children. In Walker E. and Roberts M. (eds) *Handbook of Clinical Child Psychology*. New York: Wiley.

Clark, M.M. (1971) Severe reading difficulty: a community study. *British Journal of Educational Psychology*, 41,1: 14–18.

Clarke, A.M. and Clarke, A.D.B (1976) *Early Experience: Myth and Evidence*. New York: Free Press.

Clemow, L.P. (1984) Psychological factors in childhood illness. In Adams H. and Sutker, P. (eds) *Comprehensive Handbook of Psychopathology*. New York: Plenum.

Cleveland Report (1988) CM 412. Government White Paper. HMSO.

Cloward, R. and Ohlin, L. (1969) *Delinquency and Opportunity*. Glencoe, Ill.: Free Press.

Collins, S. (1988) *Step-parents and their Children*. London: Souvenir Press.

Cooper, M. (1986) A model of persistent school absenteeism. *Educational Research*, 28, 1: 14–20.

Cornwall, K., Hedderley, R. and Pumfrey, P. (1984) Specific Learning Difficulties: The 'Specific Reading Difficulties' versus 'Dyslexia' Controversy Resolved? *British Psychological Society Working Party Report*.

Creak, M. (1961) The schizophrenic syndrome in childhood. *British Medical Journal*, 2: 889–890.

Crisp, A.H., Kalucy, R.S., Lacey, J.H. and Harding, B. (1977) The long-term prognosis in anorexia nervosa. In Vegersky, R.A. (ed.) *Anorexia Nervosa*. New York: Raven Press.

Crisp, A.H. (1980) *Anorexia Nervosa: Let Me Be*. London: Academic Press.

Crook, W.G. (1980) Can what a child eats make him dull, stupid or hyperactive? *Journal of Learning Disabilities*, 13: 281–286.

Cruickshank, W.M. (1961) *A Teaching Method for Brain Injured and Hyperactive Children.* New York: Syracuse University Press.

Cytryn, L. and McKnew, D.H. (1972) Proposed classification of childhood depression. *American Journal of Psychiatry,* 129: 63–68.

Dalley (1984) *Art as Therapy.* London: Tavistock.

Dally, P.J. (1969) *Anorexia Nervosa.* New York: Grune and Stratton.

David, D.J. (1974) Association between lower level lead concentrations and hyperactivity in children. *Environmental Health Perspectives,* 7: 17–25.

Department of Education and Science (1967) *Children and their Primary Schools* (The Plowden Report). London: HMSO.

Department of Education and Science (1978) *Special Educational Needs* (The Warnock Report). HMSO.

Department of Education and Science (1985) *Education for All* (The Swan Report). HMSO.

Department of Education and Science (1988) *Working Together for the Protection of Children From Abuse*: Procedures within the Education Service. Circular No. 4/88.

Department of Education and Science (1989) *Discipline in Schools: Report of the Committee of Enquiry* (The Elton Report). HMSO.

Department of Education and Science (1989) Circular No. 5. *Implementing the National Curriculum – Participation by Pupils with Special Educational Needs.* York: National Curriculum Council.

Department of Education and Science (1989) *Survey of Provision for pupils with EBD.* HMSO.

DES HMI (1990) *A survey of the education of children living in temporary accommodation.* DES Publications Despatch Centre, Honeypot Lane, Stanmore, Middlesex HA7 1AZ.

Docker-Drysdale, B. (1968) *Therapy in Child Care.* London: Longmans, Green.

Doleys, D.M. (1983) Enuresis and encopresis. In Ollendick, T.H. and Helsen, M. (eds) *Handbook of Child Psychopathology.* New York: Plenum.

Dollinger, S.J. (1983) Childhood Neuroses. In Walker, E. and Roberts, M. (eds) *Handbook of Clinical Child Psychology.* New York: Wiley.

Dowling, E. and Taylor, D. (1985) *The Family and the School.* London: Routledge and Kegan Paul.

Dunn, J. and Kendrick, C. (1981) Social behaviour of young siblings in the family context. *Child Development,* 52: 1265–1273.

DSM 111: (1980) American Psychiatric Association.

Eisenberg, L. and Waller, D. (1980) *School Refusal in Childhood.* Chichester: John Wiley.

Elliott, M. (1988) *Keeping Safe.* London: Hodder and Stoughton.

Erikson, E.H. (1963) *Childhood and Society* (2nd edition). New York: Norton.

Eysenck, H.J. (1947) *Dimensions of Personality.* London: Routledge and Kegan Paul.

Eysenck, H. (1990) Reported in *Education Today,* No. 2, Vol. 40.

Farley, F.A. (1973) *A Theory of Delinquency.* American Psychological Association.

Farrington, D. (1980) The Cambridge Study. In Hersov, L. and Berg, I. (eds) *Out of School.* London: Wiley.

Farrington, D.P. (1978) The family backgrounds of aggressive youths. In Hersov, L.A., Berger M. and Shaffer, D. (eds) *Aggression and Anti-social Behaviour in Childhood.* Oxford: Pergamon.

Feingold, B.F. (1968) Recognition of food additives as a cause of symptoms of allergy. *Annals of Allergy,* 26: 309–313.

Feingold, B.F. (1973) *Introduction to Clinical Allergy.* Springfield, Ill.: Thomas.

Feingold, B.F. (1973) *Adverse reaction to food additives.* New York: American Medical Association.

Fenwick, A. (1986) At the beat of the drum. *British Society For Music Therapy,* 5.

Forward, S. and Buck, C. (1981) *Betrayal of Innocence: Incest and its Devastation.* Harmondsworth: Penguin.

Freud, A. (1946) *The Psychoanalytical Treatment of Children.* London: Imago.

Freud, A. (1981) A psychoanalyst's view of sexual abuse by parents. In Mrazek, P.B. and Kempe, C.H. (eds) *Sexually Abused Children and their Families.* Oxford: Pergamon Press.

Freud, S. (1933) *Collected Papers.* London: Hogarth.

Freud, S. (1940 First German Edition) (1964) *An Outline of Psychoanalysis.* In Standard Edition, Vol 23. London: Hogarth Press.

Fritz, G.S., Stoll, K. and Wagner, N.N. (1981) A comparison of males and females who were sexually molested as children. *Journal of Sex and Marital Therapy,* 7: 54–59.

Frude, N. (1980) *Psychological Approaches to Child Abuse.* London: Batsford Academic and Educational Ltd.

Furman, R. (1969) *The Therapeutic Nursery School.* New York: International University Press.

Furman, J. and Pratt, J. (1985) *A support group for bereaved adolescents.* Paper presented to National Association of Social Workers.

Furneaux, B. and Roberts, B. (1977) *Autistic Children.* London: Routledge and Kegan Paul.

Galdston, R. (1975) Preventing the abuse of little children. *American Journal of Orthopsychiatry,* 45, 3: 372–381.

Galloway, D. (1983) Disruptive pupils and effective pastoral care. *School Organisation,* 3, 245–54.

Galloway, D. (1985) *Schools, Pupils and Special Educational Needs.* Dover: Croom Helm.

Galloway, D. (1986) Should truants be treated? *Maladjustment and Therapeutic Education.* 4, 3: 18–24.

Galloway, D. and Goodwin, C. (1979) *Educating Slow-learning and Maladjusted Children.* London: Longman.

Galloway, D. *et al.* (1985) Meeting special educational needs in the ordinary

166

school? Or creating them? *Maladjustment and Therapeutic Education*, 3, 3, 3–10.

Galloway, D. and Goodwin, C. (1987) *The Education of Disturbing Children: Pupils with Learning and Adjustment Difficulties*. London: Longmans.

Gesell, A. and Ilg, F.L. (1949) *The Child From Five to Ten*. New York: Harper.

Gesell, A., Ilg, F.L. and Ames, L.B. (1956) *Youth: The Years From Ten to Sixteen*. New York: Harper.

Gibbons, D.C. (1976) *Delinquent Behaviour*. Englewood Cliffs, N.J.: Prentice-Hall.

Gilchrist, R. (1977) Ten Dollars . . . for going to school. *Daily Mail*. 13 December 1977.

Gold, M. and Petronio, R.J. (1980) Delinquent behaviour in adolescence. In Adelson J. (ed) *Handbook of Adolescent Psychology*. New York: Wiley.

Goodwin, J. (1981) Suicide attempts in sexual abuse victims and their mothers. *Child Abuse and Neglect*, 5: 217–221.

Goodyer, I. (1981) Hysterical conversion reactions in childhood. *Journal of Child Psychology and Psychiatry*, 22: 179–188.

Gottesman, I.I. (1983) Pearls and perils in epigenetic psychopathology. *Childhood Psychopathology and Development*. New York: Raven.

Graham, J. (1988) *Schools, Disruptive Behaviour and Delinquency*. Home Office Research Study No. 96. HMSO.

Graham, P.J. (1979) Epidemiological studies. In Quay, H.C. and Werry, J.S. (eds) *Psychopathological Disorders of Childhood*. New York: Wiley.

Green, A.H. (1968) Self destructive behaviour in physically abused, schizophrenic children. *General Psychiatry*, 19: 171–179.

Grieger, T., Kauffman, J.M. and Grieger, R.M. (1976) Effects of peer reporting on cooperative play and aggression of kindergarten children. *Journal of School Psychology*, 14: 307–313.

Gutfreund, R. (1975) Resolving the Problem. *Youth in Society* May/June 1975: 12–15.

Halmi, K.A. (1985). The diagnosis and treatment of anorexia nervosa. In Shaffer, D., Erhardt A.A. and Greenhill L. (eds) *The Clinical Guide to Child Psychiatry*. New York: The Free Press.

Hanko, G. (1989) Sharing Expertise: Developing the Consultative Role. In Evans, R. (ed.) *Response to Special Educational Needs: Progress in Policy and Practice*.

Hanko, G. (1989) After Elton – How will we manage disruption? *Journal of Special Education*.

Hare, J., Sugarwara, A. and Pratt, C. (1986) The child in grief: implications for teaching. *Early Child Development and Care*, 25, 43–56.

Hargreaves, D.H. (1967) *Social Relations in a Secondary School*. London: Routledge and Kegan Paul.

Harley, J.P., Matthews, C.G. and Eichman, P. (1978) Synthetic food colours and hyperactivity in children: A double-blind challenge experiment. *Pediatrics*, 62: 975–983.

167

Harrop, L.A. (1983) *Behaviour Modification in the Classroom*. London: Hodder & Stoughton.

Hegarty, S. and Pocklington, K.ʼ (1981) *Educating Pupils with Special Needs in the Ordinary School*. Windsor: NFER-Nelson.

Herbert, M. (1982) *Conduct Disorders of Childhood and Adolescence*. New York: Wiley.

Hersov, L.A. (1960) Persistent non-attendance at school. *Journal Child Psychology*, 1: 130–136.

Hetherington, E.M. and Martin, B. (1979) Family interaction. In Quay, H.C. and Werry, J.S. (eds) *Psychopathological Disorders of Childhood*. New York: Wiley.

Hewett, F.M. and Taylor, F.D. (1980) *The Emotionally Disturbed Child in the Classroom*. Boston: Allyn and Bacon.

Hewitt, P. and Rose-Neil, W. (1990) *Your Second Baby*. London: Unwin Hyman.

Hoghughi, M. *et al. Treating Problem Children*. London: Sage Publications.

Hollingsworth, C.E., Tanguay, P.E., Grossman, L. and Pabst, P. (1980) Long term outcome of obsessive-compulsive disorder in children. *Journal of the American Academy of Child Psychiatry*, 19: 134–144.

Holmes, T.H. and Rahe, R.H. (1967) The social readjustment rating scale. *Journal of Psychosomatic Research*, 11: 213–218.

Johnson, J.H., Rasbury, W.C. and Siegal, L.J. (1986) *Approaches to Child Treatment*. Oxford: Pergamon.

Johnston, L., Bachman, J.G. and O'Malley, P. (1981) *Highlights From Student Drug Use in America*. Rockville, M.D: National Institute on Drug Abuse.

Jones, O.C. (1977) The fate of abused children. In Franklin, A.W. (ed.) *The Challenge of Child Abuse*. Yale University Press.

Judd, L.L. (1965) Obsessive compulsive disorders in children. *Archives of General Psychiatry*, 12: 136–143.

Kahn, J.H., Nursten, J.P. and Carroll, H.C.M. (1981) *Unwillingly to School*. Oxford: Pergamon.

Kandel, D.B. (1982) Epidemiological and psychosocial perspectives on adolescent drug abuse. *Journal of American Academy of Child Psychiatry*, 21: 328–347.

Kanner, L. (1943) Autistic disturbances of affective contact. *Nervous Child*, 2: 217–250.

Kashani, J. and Simonds, J.F. (1979) The incidence of depression in children. *American Journal of Psychiatry*, 136: 1203–1204.

Kashani, J.H., Barbero, G.J. and Bolander, F.D. (1981) Depression in hospitalized pediatric patients. *Journal of the American Academy of Child Psychiatry*, 20: 123–134.

Kelly, E.W. (1973) School phobia: review of theory and treatment. *Psychology in the Schools*, 10: 33–41.

Kelly, G.A. (1955) *The Psychology of Personal Constructs*. New York: Norton.

Kempe, R.S. and Kempe, C.H. (1978) *Child Abuse*. London: Fontana.

168

Kempe, C.H., Silverman, F.N., Steele, B.F., Droegmueller, W. and Silver, H.K. (1962) The battered child syndrome. *Journal of the American Medical Association*, Vol. 181, no. 17.

Kennedy, W.A. (1965) School phobia: rapid treatment of fifty cases. *Journal of Abnormal Psychology*, 70: 285–289.

Kessler, J.W. (1972) Neurosis in childhood. In Wolman, B.B. (ed.) *Manual of Child Psychopathology*. New York: McGraw-Hill.

Klein, M. (1932) *Psychoanalysis of Children*. New York: Norton.

Kohlberg, L. (1981). *Essays on Moral Development* (vol. 1). New York: Harper and Row.

Krementz, J. (1983) *How it Feels When a Parent Dies*. London: Victor Gollancz Ltd.

Kubler-Ross, E. (1983) *On Children and Death*. New York: Macmillan.

Laing, R.D. (1970) *Knots*. Harmondsworth: Penguin Books Ltd.

Lane, B.A. (1980) The relationship between learning disabilities and juvenile delinquency: current status. *Journal of Learning Disabilities*, 13: 20–30.

Lane, D.A. (1990) *The Impossible Child*. Stoke-on-Trent: Trentham Books.

Lane, H. (1928) *Talks to Parents and Teachers*. London: Allen and Unwin.

Laslett, R. and Smith, C. (1984) *Effective Classroom Management*. London: Nichols; Croom Helm.

Laslett, R. (1980) Bullies: a children's court in a day school for maladjusted children. *Journal of Special Education*, 4, 4: 391–397.

Lawrence, J., Steed, D. and Young, P. (1984) *Disruptive Children – Disruptive Schools*. London: Routledge.

Lennox, D.H. (1982) *Residential Group Therapy for Children*. London: Tavistock.

Lipowski, Z.J. (1984) What does the word 'psychosomatic' really mean? *Psychosomatic Medicine*, 46: 153–169.

Loney, J. (1983) Research diagnostic criteria for childhood hyperactivity. In Guze, S.B. (ed.) *Childhood Psychopathology and Development*. New York: Raven.

Lorenz, K. (1966) *On Aggression*. New York: Harcourt Brace Jovanovich.

Lowden, G. (1984) In Williams, P. (ed.) *Special Education in Minority Communities*. Milton Keynes: Open University Press.

Lubar, J.F. and Shouse, M.N. (1977) Use of bio-feedback in the treatment of seizure disorders and hyperactivity. In Lahey, B. and Kazdin, A. (eds.) *Advances in Clinical Child Psychology*. New York: Plenum.

Lumsden, C.J. and Wilson, E.D. (1983) *Promethean Fire*. Cambridge, Mass: Harvard University Press.

McMahon, R.C. (1980) Genetic etiology in the hyperactive child syndrome: A critical review. *American Journal of Othopsychiatry*, 50: 145–149.

McManus, M. (1989) *Troublesome Behaviour in the Classroom*. London: Routledge.

Mahler, M.S. and Turer, M. (1960) Observations on research regarding the 'symbiotic syndrome' of infantile psychosis. *Psychoanalytic Quarterly*, 29: 317–327.

Mahler, M. (1968) *On Human Symbiosis*. New York: International University Press.

Maloney, M.J. (1980) Diagnosing hysterical conversion reactions in children. *The Journal of Paediatrics*, 97: 1016-1020.

Marcoux, Y. and Kielt, M. (1985) Early Loss and Adult Personality. *Bereavement Care*, Vol. 4. No. 1.

Martin, H.P. and Beezley, P. (1976) *The emotional development of abused children*. Cambridge: Bollinger.

Maslow, A. (1968) *Toward a Psychology of Being*. New York: Van Nostrand-Reinhold.

May, D. (1975) Truancy, school absenteeism and delinquency. *Scottish Education Studies*, 7,2: 97/106.

Mays, J.B. (1954) *Growing Up in the City*. Liverpool: University Press.

Megarry, J. *et al.* (eds) (1981) The Education of Minorities. In *World Year Book of Education*. London: Kogan Page.

Melamed, B.G. and Johnson, S.B. (1981) Asthma and juvenile diabetes. In Marsh, E. and Terdal, L. (eds) *Behavioural Assessment of Childhood Disorders*. New York: Guildford.

Milby, J.B., Wendorf, D. and Meredith, R.L. (1983) Obsessive compulsive disorders. In Morris, R.J. and Kratochwill, T.R. (eds) *The Practice of Child Therapy*. New York: Pergamon.

Miles, T.R. (1983) *Dyslexia*. St Albans: Granada Publishing.

Miller, L.C., Barrett, C.L. and Hampe, E. (1974) Phobias of childhood in a prescientific era. In Davids, A. (ed.) *Child Personality and Psychopathology*. New York: Wiley.

Miller, L.C. (1983) Fears and anxieties in children. In Walker, E. and Roberts, M. (eds) *Handbook of Clinical Child Psychology*. New York: Wiley.

Milner, J. and Blyth, E. (1989) *Coping With Child Sexual Abuse: A Guide for Teachers*. Longman Group UK Ltd.

Minuchin, S. (1974) *Families and Family Therapy*. Cambridge, Mass.: Harvard University Press.

Mitchell, S. and Shepherd, M. (1979) *Persistent school absenteeism in Northern Ireland*. DES N. Ireland.

Molnar, A. and Lindquist, B. (1989) *Changing Problem Behaviour in Schools*. San Francisco, CA: Jossey Bass.

Monaco, N.M. and Gaier, E.L. (1988) Differential patterns of disclosure of child abuse among boys and girls. *Early Child Development and Care*, Vol. 30: 97-103.

Monson, D. and Hart, S. (1989) *Improving Classroom Behaviour*. London: Cassell.

Moore, D.R. and Arthur, J.L. (1983) Juvenile delinquency. In Ollendick, T. and Hersen, M. (eds) *Handbook of Child Psychopathology*. New York: Plenum.

Morgan, S.B. (1986) Early childhood autism: changing perspectives. *Journal of Child and Adolescent Psychotherapy*, 3: 3-9.

Morgan, S.R. (1987) *Abuse and Neglect of Handicapped Children*. College Hill: Little Brown Co.

Morris, R.J. and Kratochwill, T.R. (1983) *Treating Children's Fears and Phobias*. Oxford: Pergamon.

Moustakis, C. E. (1956) *The Teacher and the Child*. New York: McGraw-Hill.

Mowrer, O.H. and Mowrer, W.M. (1938) Enuresis: A method for its study and treatment. *American Journal of Orthopsychiatry*, 8: 436–459.

Mrazek, P.B. and Kempe, C.H. (1981) *Sexually Abused Children and their Families*. London: Pergamon Press.

Murray-Parkes, C. and Weiss, R. (1983) *Recovery from Bereavement*. London: Basic Books.

Nash, C.L. and West, D.J. (1985) Sexual molestation of young girls: A retrospective survey. In *Sexual Victimisation*. London: Gower.

Nasjleti, M. (1980) Suffering in silence: the male incest victim. *Child Welfare*, Vol. LIX, no. 5.

National Children's Bureau (1980) *Children in Changing Families*. London: Macmillan.

Neal, J.M. and Oltmanns, T. (1980) *Schizophrenia*. New York: Wiley.

Newton, M.J., Thomson, M.E. and Richards, I.L. (1979) *Readings in Dyslexia*. Wisbech: Learning Development Aids.

O'Connor, D.J. (1986) *Glue Sniffing and Solvent Abuse*. Manchester: Boys' and Girls' Welfare Society.

O'Gorman, G. (1970) *The Nature of Childhood Autism*. London: Butterworth.

Olweus, D. (1984) Aggressors and their victims. In Frude, N. and Gault, M. (eds) *Disruptive Behaviour in Schools*. Chichester: John Wiley.

O'Moore, M. (1988) *Bullying in Schools*. Report on course/seminar. Stavanger, Norway. 2/8/87.

O'Moore, M. (1989). Bullying in Britain and Ireland: an overview. In Roland, E. and Munthe, E. (eds) *Bullying: An International Perspective*. London: David Fulton.

Oppenheimer, R., Howells, K., Palmer, R.L. and Chaloner, D.A. (1985) Adverse sexual experience in childhood and clinical eating disorders. *Journal of Psychiatric Research*, 19, 2/3: 357–361.

Palmer, R.L. (1980) Anorexia Nervosa: *A Guide for Sufferers and their Families*. London: Penguin Books.

Paulor, I.P. (1927) *Conditioned Reflexes*. London: Oxford University Press.

Peake, A. (1989) *Working with Sexually Abused Children*. London: The Children's Society.

Pearce, J. (1977) Depressive disorder in childhood. *Journal of Child Psychology and Psychiatry*, 18: 74–82.

Pervin, L.A. (1980) *Personality: Theory, Assessment and Research*. Canada: John Wiley and Sons, Inc.

Pfeffer, C.R. (1981) Suicidal behaviour of children. *American Journal of Psychiatry*, 138: 154–160.

Piaget, J. (1965) *The Moral Judgement of the Child*. New York: Free Press.

Piaget, J. (1970) Piaget's theory. In P.H. Mussen (ed.) *Carmichael's manual of child psychology* (vol. 1). New York: Wiley.

Porter, R. (ed.) *Child Sexual Abuse Within the Family*. London: Tavistock.

Purcell, K. (1969) The effects of asthma in children of experimental separation from the family. *Psychosomatic Medicine*, 31: 144–164.

171

Quay, H. C. (1964) Dimensions of personality in delinquent boys as inferred from factor analysis of case history data. *Child Development*, 35: 479–484.

Quay, H.C. (1965) *Juvenile Delinquency*. New York: Van Nostrand.

Quay, H.C. (1984) A critical analysis of DSM-111 as a taxonomy of psychopathology in childhood and adolescence. Unpublished manuscript, University of Miami.

Ratcliff, S.G. and Field, M.A. (1982) Emotional disorder in XYY children: four case reports. *Journal of Child Psychology and Psychiatry*, 23: 401–406.

Redl, F. and Wineman, D. (1952) *Controls from Within*. New York: Macmillan.

Reid, K. (1982) The self-concept and persistent school absenteeism. *British Journal of Educational Psychology* 52, 2: 179–187.

Reid, K. (1983) Institutional factors and persistent school absenteeism. *Educational Management and Administration*, 11, 1: 17-27.

Reid, K. (1984). Some social, psychological and educational aspects related to persistent school absenteeism. *Research in Education*, 31: 63/82.

Reid, K. (1986) *Disaffection from School*. London: Methuen.

Reynolds, D., Jones, D., Leger, S. and Murgatroyd, D. (1980) School factors and truancy. In Hersov, L. and Bers, I. (eds) *Out of School*. London: Wiley.

Righton, P. (1981) The Adult. In Taylor, B. (ed.) *Perspectives on Paedophilia*. London: Batsford Academic.

Rimm, D.C., and Masters, J.C. (1972) *Behaviour Therapy: Techniques and Empirical Findings*. New York: Academic Press.

Robins, L.N. (1966) *Deviant Children Grown Up*. Baltimore: Williams and Wilkins.

Robins, L. and Ratcliff, K. (1980) The long term outcome of truancy in Hersov, L. and Berg, I. (eds) *Out of School*. Chichester: John Wiley.

Rogers, C.R. (1957) The necessary and sufficient conditions of therapeutic personality change. *Journal of Consulting Psychology*, 21: 95–104.

Rogers, C.R. (1961) *On Becoming a Person*. Boston, Mass.: Houghton Mifflin.

Roland, E. (1988) Bullying: the Scandinavian research tradition. In Tattum, D. and Lane, D. (eds) *Bullying in Schools*. Trentham: Trentham Books.

Rosenn, D.W. (1982) Suicidal behaviour in children and adolescents. In Bassuk, E., Schoonover, S.C. and Gill, A.D. (eds) *Lifelines: Clinical Perspectives on Suicide*. New York: Plenum.

Rutter, M. (1967) A children's behaviour questionnaire for completion by teachers. *Journal of Child Psychology and Psychiatry*, 8: 1–11

Rutter, M. (1972) Parent-child separation: Psychological effects on children. *Journal of Child Psychology and Psychiatry*, 12: 233-260.

Rutter, M. (1978) Diagnosis and definition. In Rutter, M. and Schopler, E. *Autism – a Reappraisal of Concepts and Treatments*. New York: Plenum Press.

Rutter, M. (1979) Maternal deprivation. *Child Development*, 50: 283-305.

Rutter, M., Tizard, J. and Whitmore, K. (1970) *Education, Health and Behaviour*. London: Longman.

Rutter, M., Cox, A., Tupling, C., Berger, M. and Yule, W. (1975). Attainment and adjustment in two geographical areas. *British Journal of Psychiatry*, 126: 493–509.

Rutter, M., Maughan, B., Mortimore, P. and Ouston, J. (1979). *Fifteen Thousand Hours*. Wells, Somerset: Open Books Publishing Ltd.

Sandberg, A.A. (1961) XYY human male. *Lancet*, 2: 488–489.

Saunders, M. (1979) *Class Control and Behaviour Problems*. Maidenhead: McGraw-Hill.

Schwartz, S. and Johnson, J.H. (1985) *Psychopathology of Childhood*. Oxford: Pergamon.

Shannon, W.R. (1922) Neuropathic manifestations in infants and children as a result of anaphylactic reactions to food contained in their diet. *American Journal of Diseases in Children*, 24: 89–94.

Shaw, C.R. and McKay, H.D. (1969) *Juvenile Delinquency in Urban Areas*. Chicago: University of Chicago Press.

Skinner, B.F. (1953) *Science and Human Behaviour*. New York: Macmillan.

Staudacher, C. (1988) *Beyond Grief*. London: Souvenir Press.

Stephenson, P. and Smith, D. (1989) Bullying in the junior school. In Tattum, D. and Lane, D. (eds) *Bullying in Schools*. Trentham: Trentham Books.

Sternberg, F. and Sternberg, B. (1980). *If I Die and When I Do*. Englewood Cliffs, N.J: Prentice-Hall.

Storr, A. (1970) *Human Aggression*. Harmondsworth: Penguin.

Stott, D. (1982) *Helping the Maladjusted Child*. Milton Keynes: Open University Press.

Surkes, S. (1988) Truants are destined for the dole. *Times Educational Supplement* 3775: 5.

Tansley, P. and Panckhurst, J. (1981) *Children with Specific Learning Difficulties*. Windsor: NFER- Nelson.

Tatelbaum, J. (1980) *The Courage to Grieve*. London: Cedar Books.

Tattum, D. (1989) Bullying – a problem crying out for attention. *Pastoral Care*, 6/89: 21–25.

Taylor, L., Lacey, R. and Bracken, D. (1979). *In Whose Best Interests?* London: The Cobden Trust/MIND.

Thornbury, R. (1978) *The Changing Urban School*. London: Methuen.

Thornton, V. (1981) Growing up with cerebral palsy. In Moseby *Sexuality and Physical Disability*. London: Routledge.

Tinbergen, N. and Tinbergen, E.A. (1983) *Autistic Children – New Hope for a Cure*. London: Allen and Unwin.

Tizard, B. and Hodges, J. (1978) The effect of early institutional rearing on the development of eight-year old children. *Journal of Child Psychology and Psychiatry*, 19: 99–118.

Tresidder, E. (1986) Clues from the Class Register. *Concern*, 61: 13–15.

Tsai, M., Feldman-Summers, S. and Edgar, M. (1979) Childhood molestation. *Journal of Abnormal Psychology*, 88: 407–417.

Tyne and Wear Study (1983) In O'Connor, D.J. *Glue Sniffing and Solvent Abuse*. Cheadle: Boys and Girls Welfare Society.

173

Underwood Report (1955) Ministry of Education Report of the Committee on Maladjusted Children.

Van Eerdewegh, M.M. *et al.* (1982) The Bereaved Child. *British Journal of Psychiatry*, 140: 23-29.

Waller, D. and Eisenberg, L. (1980) School refusal in childhood – a psychiatric-paediatric perspective. In Hersor, L. and Berg, I. (eds) *Out of School*. London: Wiley.

Ward, E. (1984) *Father – Daughter Rape*. London: The Women's Press.

Ward, J. (1971) Modification of children's deviant classroom behaviour. *British Journal of Educational Psychology*, 41.

Watson, J.B. (1913) Psychology as the behaviourist views it. *Psychological Review*, 20: 158-177.

Watson, J.B. (1928) *Psychological Care of Infant and Child*. New York: Norton.

Weathers, L. and Liberman, R.P. (1975) The family contracting exercise. *The Journal of Behaviour Therapy and Experimental Psychiatry*, 6: 208-214.

Wedge, P. and Essen, J. (1982) *Children in Adversity*. London: Pan.

Welch, M. (1988) *Rescue from Autism*. BBC television (November).

Werry, J.S. (1972) Psychosomatic disorders. In Quay, H.C. and Werry, J.S. (eds) *Psychopathological Disorders in Childhood*. New York: Wiley.

Wheldall, K. and Glynn, T. (1989) *Effective Classroom Learning*. Oxford: Blackwell Ltd.

Wheldall, K. and Merrett, E. (1987) *The Behaviourist in the Classroom*. London: Allen and Unwin.

Widlake, P. (1983) *How to Reach the Hard to Teach*. Milton Keynes: Open University Press.

Wilson, D. and Gillham, B. (1986) *Handicapping Conditions in Children*. Association for Handicapped Adults and Children.

Wing, J.K., O'Connor, N. and Lotter, V. (1967) Autistic conditions in early childhood: a survey in Middlesex. *British Medical Journal*, 3: 389-392.

Wing, L. (1976) *Early Childhood Autism*. Oxford: Pergamon.

Wolfson, R. (1989) Bullying at school. *Health at School*, 4: 2/89.

Wolpe, J. and Lazarus, A.A. (1966) *Behaviour Therapy Techniques: A Guide to the Treatment of Neuroses*. New York: Pergamon.

Yates, A. (1982) Children eroticized by incest. *American Journal of Psychiatry*, 139(4): 482-485.

York, R., Heron, J.M. and Wolff, S. (1972) Exclusion from school. *Journal of Child Psychology and Psychiatry*, 13: 259-266.

Yule, W., Hersov, L. and Treseder, J. (1980) Behavioural treatment in school refusal. In Hersov, L. and Berg I. (eds) *Out of School*. London: Wiley.

Zapella, M. (1979) *Il Bambino Nella Luna*. Milan: Feltrinelli.

Zarkowska, E. and Clements, J. (1988) *Problem Behaviour in People with Severe Learning Disabilities*. Beckenham: Croom Helm.

Zentall, S. (1975) Optimal stimulation as theoretical basis of hyperactivity. *American Journal of Orthopsychiatry*, 45: 549-563.

Index

'abnormal' behaviour 9, 21
absence from school:
  see truancy
abuse:
  see child abuse, ritual abuse, sexual
    abuse
Achenbach, T. M. 11
adolescence 63
agression (child) 140–2
  bullying and 156
alcohol 88–90 *passim*
anorexia nervosa 78–9
anxiety disorders 95–8
Arora, C. 158
art therapy 50
asthma (childhood) 74–7
attention deficit disorder (ADD) 85–8
autism:
  see early infantile autism
avoidant disorders 97–8

bed-wetting 81
behavioural approaches (EBD) 19–22
  to delinquency 154
  to hysteria 107
see also operant conditioning, positive
  reinforcement
behavioural difficulties:
  see EBD
bereavement 51–2
Berg, I. 101
Blyth, E. 129
Bowlby, J. 53
brain pathology 82

bulimia (nervosa) 78–9
bullying 103, 155–9

Charles, J. 122
child abuse 116–38
  physical abuse 118–24
  sexual abuse 39–42 *passim*, 79,
    124–37
child neglect 118, 122
Children Act (1989) 47, 68, 69
Children's Behaviour Questionnaire
  12–14
classification systems (EBD) 10–14
  critique of 14
cognitive (development) theory 35–8
Collins, Stephen 49
compulsions 104–5
conduct disorders 139–59
confrontation (teacher–pupil) 148–9
conversion reactions 106–7
Cooper, M. 63
counselling:
  see pastoral care
Crook, W. G. 16
cross-cultural issues 60–2
curricular issues 26, 38
  child abuse and 136–7
  truancy and 66
death 52
  see also bereavement, grieving
    process, loss in childhood
delinquency:
  see juvenile delinquency
depression (childhood) 107–10

development psychology 30–42
  biological theories 32–5
  cognitive theory 35–8
  psychodynamic theories 38–41
diet 16
disasters 47–8
disclosure (of sexual abuse) 134–6
disruption 142–51
drug abuse 88–92
DSM-III 10–11
  attention deficit/hyperactivity 85–6
  conduct disorders 139–40
  depression 108
dyslexia 83–5

early infantile autism 111–12, 114
eating problems 77–9
EBD (emotional and behavioural
      difficulties) 5–14, 160–1
  aetiology and treatment of 15–29
  child abuse 116–38
  classification of 10–14
  conduct disorders 139–59
  defined 2–3, 7–10
  and development psychology 30–42
  and environmental stress 43–55
  and physical conditions 73–94
  psychoneurotic disorders 95–110
  psychotic disorders 110–5
  truancy 56–72

ecological approach (EBD) 22–8
Education Reform Act (1988) 3–4
elimination problems 80–1
Elliott, Michelle 137
Elotn Committee Report 139–47
    passim, 150, 160–1
emotional difficulties:
  see EBD
encropresis 82
enuresis 81
environmental management (EBD)
    25–6
environmental stress 43–55
epilepsy 76–7
Erikson, E. H. 29

ethnic minorities:
  see cross-cultural issues
ethology 32, 34
Eysenck, H. 8

family circumstances:
  see home circumstances, one-parent
    families
family therapy techniques 24
fears (childhood) 98–104
  see also anxiety disorders
Feingold, B. F. 16
Freud, S. 38–40 passim
Frude, N. 119

Galloway, D. 71, 146
genetic inheritance 16–17
  delinquency and 152–3
  and psychological development 32–4
Gesell, Arnold 32–3
Goodyer, I. 106, 107
grieving process 51, 53–4

Holmes, T. H. 43
home circumstances 24, 27–8, 43–52
  asthma and 75
  truancy and 58–62 passim
homelessness 46–7
homosexual relationships 48
hyperactivity 85–8
hysteria (childhood) 105–7

inheritance:
  see genetic inheritance
internalising–externalising symptoms 11

Johnston, L. 89
juvenile delinquency 151–5

Kanner, L. 111
Kennedy, W. A. 103–4
Kidscape charity 132, 136, 156
Kohlberg, L. 37–8

Lawrence, J. 145
learning difficulties 3
  delinquency and 153–4

specific 83–5
see also specific learning difficulties
Lipowski, Z. J. 74
loss in childhood 48–9, 51–3
Lowden, G. 60

McManus, M. 148–9
maladjustment 2
  definitions of 7–10
maturation, theory of 32
Mays, J. B. 60
Medical Model (EBD) 15–17
Miller, L. C. 98–9
Milner, J. 129
modelling (Bandura) 20
moral development 35–8
mourning process:
  see grieving process
Moustakis, C. E. 8
music therapy 50

National Curriculum 27
neglect:
  see child neglect
neurotic disorders 95–110
Newpin charity 119–20

obsessions 104–5
one-parent families 48–51
operant conditioning 20
  for agression 142

paedophilia 130
pastoral care
  bereavement and 54
  disaster and 47–8
  phobias and 99
  solvent abuse and 93
  truancy and 71
phobias 20, 21, 98–104
  school 20, 100–4
Piaget, J. 29, 35–7
play therapy 50
positive reinforcement 21, 69
  of non-agressive behaviour 142
psychodrama 49

psychodynamic approach:
  EBD 17–19
  psychological development 38–41
psychoneuroses:
  see neurotic disorders
psychosis (childhood) 110–15
psychosomatic disorders 73–4

Quay, H. C. 11, 151–2

Rahe, R. H. 43
reading difficulties 83–4
Reid, K. 59
relaxation exercise 100
ritual abuse 131–2
Rogers, C. R. 29
Roland, E. 156

Samaritans, 109–10
schizophrenia (childhood) 113–15
school phobia 20, 100–4
separation disorders 97–8
sexual abuse 39–42 *passim*, 124–37
  anorexia and 79
sexual development 38–41 *passim*
sibling rivalry 46
sleep problems 80
Smith, D. 157
solvent abuse 92–3
somatoform disorders 105–7
Special Educational Needs (SEN) 3–4
specific learning difficulties (SLD) 83–5
  see also learning difficulties
Stephenson, P. 157
step-parent families 49
Stott, Denis 50–1
stress:
  see environmental stress
suicide (child) 109
symbiotic psychosis 113, 114
systematic desensitisation 20, 21, 105
  for phobias 99, 104
systems approach:
  see ecological approach

Tantelbaum, J. 53
tobacco 88–90 *passim*

Transactional Analysis 29
truancy 56–72
  dealing with 67–72
  defined 58
  school factors in 64–7

underachievement 62
Underwood Committee 2, 7–8

Warnock (Committee) Report 3

Watson, John B. 19–20
'whole-school' approach 23, 46, 67,
  150
  bullying and 157–9 *passim*

Yule, W. 101–2

Zentall, S. 87–8